Medical Law: A Very Short Introduction

For more information visit our web site
www.oup.com/vsi/

Charles Foster

MEDICAL LAW

A Very Short Introduction

OXFORD
UNIVERSITY PRESS

OXFORD
UNIVERSITY PRESS

Great Clarendon Street, Oxford, OX2 6DP,
United Kingdom

Oxford University Press is a department of the University of Oxford.
It furthers the University's objective of excellence in research, scholarship,
and education by publishing worldwide. Oxford is a registered trade mark of
Oxford University Press in the UK and in certain other countries

First Edition published in 2013

Impression: 3

British Library Cataloguing in Publication Data
Data available

ISBN 978-0-19-966044-5

Printed in Great Britain by
Ashford Colour Press Ltd, Gosport, Hampshire

Contents

Acknowledgements

Every book is a piece of plagiarism—a mosaic of the ideas of others. This is probably particularly true of law books. All an author can do is to rearrange the ideas into a new-ish form, and do some processing. Often the sources are impossible to trace. A source might be a raised eyebrow in a seminar, or the tone of a sentence. So every list of acknowledgements is both incomplete and invidious. Here, however, are some of the people to whom I know I owe a great debt:

Jonathan Herring, Tony Hope, Mike Parker, Julian Savulescu, Richard Ashcroft, Roger Brownsword, Aharon Barak, Mikey Dunn, Mark Sheehan, Dom Wilkinson, John Keown, John Tingle, Jane Kaye, a host of barristers who've pointed out my misconceptions both gently and aggressively, OUP's anonymous reviewers, and the Principal, Fellows, and students of Green Templeton College, Oxford.

I don't know why authors always feel the need to say that all remaining errors are their own. I've always been taught not to state the blindingly obvious, and so I won't.

Charles Foster
Green Templeton College
University of Oxford
April 2012

List of illustrations

Chapter 1
Origins and legacies

As a discrete subject, medical law is young. But regulation of the medical profession is not. Being able to hack into people's bodies for money is a remarkable privilege, and it entails particular responsibility. It has long been recognized (even if it is being quickly forgotten) that medicine isn't like any other business. An orthopaedic surgeon might have the same skills as a carpenter, but bone and muscle were and are regarded as being made of stuff importantly, if mysteriously, different from pine and plywood. Bone and flesh build boxes for souls. Mess with the boxes and you could affect the soul. That gives physicians and surgeons awesome, high-priestly power.

The accountability of medicine's high priests

Priests are a set-apart caste: they are expected to behave better than the hoi polloi. All priests serve in temples. Those in the temples dedicated to divinities are answerable to the divinities; and those (the doctors) who serve in the material temples of the human soul (by rummaging around inside chests or by putting leeches on limb stumps) are answerable to the body owners, or to the society that represents them. But there is a problem about such accountability. If you're an inaccessibly high high priest—if your work is beyond the ken of the people to whom you're accountable—how can accountability be real?

The doctors persuaded the people that they, the doctors, had to regulate themselves on behalf of the people. The Hippocratic Oath, already extant in the 5th century BCE (and therefore probably borrowed by the Hippocratic School from some mystical Pythagorean ancestors), is the classic example. It's a code drawn up by doctors, for doctors, and is policed, more or less, by doctors.

For most of the next two and a half millennia, the Hippocratic Oath, or one of its many variants, has been the law regulating the medical profession. But here's the point: these codes are not laws in the usual sense of the world. They are sets of ethical principles: the rules of a very exclusive club. Only when self-regulation manifestly failed, or the law acquired a self-confidence it has rarely had, or it became politically desirable to question the propriety of self-rule by an esoteric elite, did the law think it either necessary or appropriate to intrude into the holy of holies where the white-coated, bloodstained priests stood with their votive knives.

By and large, continental Europe, was quicker to regulate doctors than were England, the British Commonwealth, or the US, but it is hard to generalize usefully about why this was. Both France and Germany, for instance, imposed legal duties of confidentiality on doctors far earlier than did Britain, but their motives for doing so were not necessarily the same. Catholic France was perhaps influenced by the analogy between the confessional and the consulting room. If so, the French duty of confidence might be an affirmation of the sanctity of the consultation rather than the human rights of the patient. Germany, on the other hand, has always been keener than many nations on regulation for regulation's sake. But everywhere, until the middle of the 20th century, medical practitioners enjoyed extraordinary social status, and a legal status bordering unacceptably on immunity.

1. Hippocrates (c.460–c.370 BCE), the 'Father of Western Medicine', who is (probably wrongly) credited with the formulation of the Hippocratic Oath, a declaration of ethical principles on which subsequent medical regulatory codes have drawn

The Nazis changed this. Their doctors showed that a professional qualification did not imply a decent conscience.

The seeds of this recognition were sown in the French Revolution and the Great War, when the myth of the infallibility of the upper orders was comprehensively and bloodily exploded. But it's one thing to realize that a moustachioed, titled general is an ass. It's another to recognize that a doctor, pledged professionally to heal, and speaking words of fate in hermetic language, might be incompetent or downright evil. It took Mengele to teach the world that doctors couldn't be trusted to regulate themselves. This was an important moment for the rule of law.

The world learned quickly. Immediately after World War II there was a proliferation of international declarations and professional codes, including the Declaration of Geneva, 1947 (revised 1968 and 1983) and the World Medical Association's international code of medical ethics, 1949 (revised 1968 and 1983).

This change in the *zeitgeist*, crystallized in and evidenced by the codes, was fairly effective in regulating unconscionable conduct (although, as we'll see, some abominable things still continued to happen in the world of medical research, particularly in countries and amongst populations who, it was thought, wouldn't invoke the newly promulgated, if rather toothless, declarations). It was less effective in changing judicial attitudes towards well-meaning but technically inadequate clinical conduct. Judges still tended to regard an assertion of clinical negligence as a piece of insubordination: the thin end of the Marxist revolutionary wedge. The judges, after all, had been to the same schools as the doctors, and drank the same ancient claret. If the professional judgement of a doctor could be questioned, where would it end? Lawyers might be next in the firing line. This led, as we see in Chapter 6, to an abuse of one of the commonest tests for establishing a breach of duty—the '*Bolam* test'. This is the idea that a doctor is not negligent if what he has done would be endorsed by a responsible

4

body of opinion in the relevant specialty. The abuse continues, although it's on the wane. Constitutional lawyers would assume, and everyone else would hope, that it was self-evident that the law, not the doctors, set the standard by which doctors should be judged. It is not yet self-evident to judges everywhere. English judges have been particularly slow learners.

A new set of medico-legal tools

When the law, belatedly, dealt with the health-care professions, it did so using tools that had been made for other things. It used notions of contract that were originally devised to regulate the sale of wool, concepts of trusteeship that worked well enough in suppressing the skulduggery of executors, and ideas of duty that let ginger beer manufacturers know where they stood if they let snails die in their bottles. These ideas do not necessarily export well into operating theatres. The chance of successful export is not increased if the export is handled (as it was) by legal practitioners (barristers, solicitors, and judges) who know a lot about the conveyance of land, the rule against perpetuities, the construction of bills of lading, and the Oxford and Cambridge Boat Race, but nothing whatever about the circulation of the blood or the anatomy of the bile ducts.

It's surprising that things worked out as well as they did. Long before it was possible to talk about a corpus of medical law, let alone a profession of medical lawyers, the courts, proceeding by more or less bad analogy with commercial and personal injury litigation, and by an instinct for fair play honed or ablated on the cricket field, did approximate justice in the relatively few medical cases that came before them.

No accurate figures exist for the number of medical cases brought in the various jurisdictions. One problem is simply that of definition. What's a 'medical case'? But whatever a medical case is, the number of them increased steadily after World War II, and then, after the 1970s, increased very rapidly indeed. The rise in the number of cases was paralleled by an increasing acknowledgement of medical law as a subject in its own right. The two acted synergistically. The more medical cases, the more law: the more law, the more public and professional recognition of the possibilities of medical litigation, and hence the more cases.

Lawyers, particularly in the US, went into a feeding frenzy. The profit motive isn't always a friend of nuance, but even greedy lawyers are sometimes clever and imaginative, and the desire to win cases and boost reputations gave the judges a chance to mould a distinctive corpus of medical law. And they did.

England typically catches American colds and ideas about ten years after the Americans are immune to them, and it is certainly true that English (and Commonwealth) medical law has borrowed some central medico-legal ideas from the US. But the medico-legal community is more genuinely international and egalitarian than many other legal communities. Everyone wants to learn from everyone else. Authorities from other jurisdictions are cited with less apology and embarrassment in medical cases than in many others. Perhaps this is because medical law deals with the most fundamental questions about humans. Americans might convey land in a different way from the Vietnamese, but they're born and they die similarly. Perhaps, too, it's because the questions are terribly difficult, being laced bracingly with biology and metaphysics. This means that judges are grateful for all the help they can get. At any rate there has been promiscuous cross-fertilization (the cynics would say cross-infection), which has produced some exciting, vigorous hybrids.

The industry of academic medical law

Another important chicken-and-egg-type question relates to the role of academic lawyers. Medical law courses have been taught now for many years, but have mushroomed over the last decade.

They have produced graduates who have gone on to swell both the numbers of medical cases litigated and the sophistication of the arguments ventilated in that litigation. This has given their old tutors more to write about, so generating a demand for more medical law textbooks and courses, and so on, if not ad infinitum, at least to the point of medical law having a recognized status both as an academic subject and a professional sub-discipline. In some ways this is a shame: respectability leads to petrifaction. There was a swashbuckling, rather rag-tag feel about medical law twenty years ago. Now medical law has a paunch, a suit, and a mortgage. You used to be able to say anything. Now there's a growing orthodoxy. When you get orthodoxy you get heresies and burnings.

Medical law and medical ethics: a tense but fecund marriage

Medical law, both in academic courses and textbook titles, often has a partner: medical ethics. The nature of the partnership is obscure and complex. Medical ethics purport to say what doctors should do: medical law purports to say what doctors should do, *or else*. But it's not so simple. There are ethical courts—the disciplinary bodies—which have fearsome teeth.

Lord Justice Hoffmann, in *Airedale NHS Trust v Bland* (1993), said: 'I would expect medical ethics to be formed by the law rather than the reverse.' At first blush it seems that he got it wrong. The influence of the *Bolam* test is profound. In many jurisdictions the liability of professionals is determined by professional peers. A clinician will not be negligent if he's done something in a way that would be endorsed by a responsible body of clinicians in the relevant specialty. Often (for instance in the law of consent and confidentiality) discussions about what amounts to legally responsible conduct have a distinctly ethical flavour. The ethical guidelines from the relevant regulatory bodies will be cited, and experts will opine about whether a rightly oriented professional conscience could reach the same conclusion as the defendant. Ethics seem to lead the way.

But is it really so? Who drafts the guidelines? Often lawyers will have sat on the relevant committees, infusing the drafts with their wisdom and folly. Lawyers are often listened to with entirely unjustified deference. Through guidelines and through dinner party conversations, lawyers may wittingly or unwittingly influence the consciences of surgeons, nurses, and occupational therapists. Hoffmann LJ didn't imagine that the law would exercise its influence like this, but he might have got it right after all.

Practising lawyers, though, tend not to be very philosophically literate or interested. And even if they are, they don't usually have time for anything other than rule-of-thumb, case-by-case-basis pragmatism. This is frustrating in the law of contract: it can be quite literally deadly in the law of medicine, where every question, properly examined, is a version of the Psalmist's: 'What is man, that thou art mindful of him?' If medical law is ruled entirely by the lawyers, it'll be a clunking, mechanistic thing. To deal properly with its astonishing subjects (humans), it needs to be more reflective, polymathic, and multilingual than it is or than it ever realistically can be. It will always fail, but it badly needs the help of the philosophers to help it fail less abjectly and more coherently.

Chapter 2
The enforcement of medical law

When health-care professionals are accused of doing something wrong, they might find themselves in jail, poverty, disgrace, or all three. This chapter maps their journeys.

The journey to jail: criminal jurisdiction

Health-care professionals can find the collars of their white coats fingered by the police for many things. They can and do sexually abuse their patients. This seems to be a particular pursuit of general practitioners/family doctors and psychiatrists, no doubt because of the opportunities that those specialities give, rather than because the specialities attract a disproportionate number of sexual predators. They invent clinically implausible excuses for breast and vaginal examinations, drug or hypnotize their patients into compliance, and misuse clinical photographs.

They can, and do, get involved in various types of medically related fraud, from fiddling their expenses or claiming for work done on non-existent patients, to drilling out and filling healthy teeth.

There's nothing quintessentially medical about the law relating to medical fraud. You can see the principles in any criminal law textbook. We meet the distinctively medical parts of sexual and other assaults in Chapter 5, on consent. But when doctors and nurses kill, the law is particular, particularly interesting, and particularly controversial.

The law of medical murder and manslaughter is dealt with in Chapter 9, on the end of life. There's of course a big and loud debate about whether the state should prosecute doctors who deliberately and compassionately 'ease the passing' of manifestly competent patients who ask for help in dying.

But what about accidental killing? Are the big guns of the criminal law appropriately directed against doctors who simply make a mistake with lethal consequences?

Take two examples:

A patient is undergoing a serious abdominal operation. Unknown and unknowable to the surgeon, the patient starts to bleed badly. The blood pressure plummets. This would be easily correctable if the anaesthetist notices. But he doesn't, since, bored by the long procedure, he's doing the crossword. The patient has a cardiac arrest and dies.

A patient has an epidural catheter placed for pain relief. She screams out for a top-up of her anaesthetic dose. A hard-pressed nurse draws up the anaesthetic and injects it. She has not checked the bottle properly. The drug is a highly toxic cancer chemotherapy agent, and the patient dies.

In both these cases the police are summoned. In both cases the family has an unanswerable claim for compensatory damages, and in both cases the clinicians involved are likely to be hauled before the relevant professional regulatory body. They may never work again. What's to be gained from criminal proceedings?

It might be said that the taking of a life is always a serious business, and must be seen to be taken seriously by the state, rather than only by the individuals most closely involved. The state exists to safeguard the security of individuals: its appearance in the role of prosecutor in criminal proceedings is part of that custodianship responsibility, and the mere fact of the prosecution (perhaps *particularly* where the forensic fuss seems out of proportion to the magnitude of the defendant's default) is shouting something important about the sanctity of human life.

Then there are the arguments which rest on what the state's responsibility entails. It entails a duty to investigate properly the deaths of its subjects (a responsibility embodied, for instance, in Article 2 of the European Convention on Human Rights). This is partly because investigation involves healthy catharsis, and partly so that the lessons of tragedy are not missed. The prevention of future fatalities is important in another way: the drama of criminal proceedings might cause other potential defaulters to be more careful.

Against all this it can be said that there are plenty of other more appropriate ways of saying that lives are important and that the state cares. In most modern states inquests or other fatality investigations discharge the investigatory and, to some extent, the cathartic functions of a criminal trial. Regulatory proceedings ensure that individual doctors learn the lessons their own sense of guilt might not have taught them, and that wider risk management lessons are disseminated to the profession as a whole. Adding yet another set of proceedings simply runs up costs that might better be spent on health care, delays the start of the grieving process, and panders to a prurient press.

And yet patients' families often want criminal proceedings. Revenge is an old and deep instinct.

The journey to poverty: civil claims for damages

Doctors are much more likely to be sued than prosecuted. The claim will typically be in the form: 'You shouldn't have done that. It's caused me damage. I want compensation.' Typical examples are negligence claims (see Chapter 6), claims based on consent (Chapter 5), and claims based on confidentiality and privacy (Chapter 4).

In most jurisdictions these claims are tried by professional judges sitting alone. Those judges may or may not have any particular expertise in medical cases, but the trend worldwide is towards judicial specialization.

There are still jurisdictions (notably the US) where civil claims are commonly tried by lay juries. This scares the life out of defendants and their insurers. If you were an accountant, how would you like your ability to prepare a balance sheet judged by an innumerate panel, none of whom knows what a balance sheet is? It's hard for the presiding judge to keep juries on a tight rein. They're easily led by their noses and heartstrings rather than by the facts.

Where (as is common in the UK) the relevant health care has been given by a public body, the public body rather than the individual doctor concerned is likely to be the defendant. But even in the UK lots of health care is provided by private doctors or by family doctors (general practitioners, or GPs) who, although paid ultimately by the state, are sued in their own name. If the private doctor or GP has paid the necessary insurance premium, and the alleged malpractice falls within the terms of the policy (sexual misconduct, for instance, may well not), the insurer will indemnify the doctor and pay his legal costs and, if he loses, those of the other side. So, generally, if he's kept up his premium payments and has been 'merely' negligent, the doctor's unlikely to lose his house.

Medical litigation is big business. And so, therefore, is professional indemnity insurance. Malpractice insurance premiums form a significant part of the total professional expenses of any doctor—and particularly those in specialties more likely to be sued (such as surgeons of various types) or in specialties likely to be sued for huge amounts of compensation (such as obstetricians, since brain-damaged babies are expensive).

A 2011 study of US doctors showed that 75 per cent of physicians in 'low-risk' specialties, and practically all in 'high-risk' specialties, would face a malpractice suit at some time in their careers. But that doesn't mean they will be successfully sued. The pattern is the same in the US as elsewhere: most claims don't result in a payment to the claimant. More detailed statistics would be meaningless: they depend crucially on the mechanics of the compensation systems in the relevant jurisdiction.

There have been strident calls for reform in many US states. Sometimes reforms have been enacted—typically along the lines of setting up special courts for malpractice litigation (on the assumption that they will deal with cases more speedily, so reducing costs, and will be less likely to be bamboozled by eloquent lawyers), reducing the length of time that a claimant has to bring a claim, and setting limits on compensation for pain, suffering, and loss of amenity (that part of the claim which is not capable of scientific-ish quantification, and which juries some- times assess in an over-sympathetic and wholly disproportionate way).

The journey to disgrace and unemployment: disciplinary and regulatory proceedings

An appearance before the profession's disciplinary tribunal is what many health-care professionals fear most. They are unlikely, unless they are depraved, monstrously careless, or very unlucky, to find themselves before a criminal court. A civil claim for damages, although troublesome and embarrassing, is dealt with by the insurers. But a complaint that is explored before the regulatory body, almost certainly in public, can have much of the stigma of criminal proceedings, and, since it may lead to removal of the right to practise, can be financially devastating.

Most jurisdictions have some sort of self-regulation of the professions. It's often done using a quasi-criminal procedure, with investigation according to standard protocols, obligations on the part of the 'prosecution' to disclose everything material to the 'defendant', detailed charges, examination and cross-examination conducted as they would be in a criminal court, and a 'sentencing' stage, with provision for testimonials and other mitigation.

Regulatory tribunals are necessarily concerned with the confidence that the public has in the profession. A sanction such as suspension from practice or erasure from the register can be imposed simply because the public is outraged. This can make regulatory tribunals a sophisticated form of lynch mob—more responsive to the media's call for a pound of flesh than they are to the rules of procedure or basic fairness. This is one reason why many of their decisions are reviewed by the courts exercising public law jurisdiction.

Public law jurisdiction

Many important decisions in medical law turn on whether a public authority (typically a local or national health-care provider) has acted lawfully. Examples might include a decision not to fund a particular type of treatment, to permit research on embryos, or to produce national guidelines setting out the criteria that should be used in deciding whether or not to withdraw life-sustaining treatment.

The way in which such questions are litigated depends very much on the quirks of the jurisdiction concerned. In the US, Germany, and South Africa, for instance, the constitution is likely to be invoked; in Israel, the basic laws. In the UK there is a broad provision for judicial review of administrative action. In the UK and other countries which are signatories of the European Convention on Human Rights, national laws or the means of their implementation can be challenged in national courts for alleged non-compliance with the Convention, with eventual recourse to the European Court of Human Rights in Strasbourg. Many cases with a medical taste have found themselves there. Many other jurisdictions have similar arrangements.

Human rights language is particularly common in medical law. It's not surprising. Medical cases often invoke the most fundamental questions we can ask about human beings, their relationship to their bodies, and their relationship to the other bodies that comprise the societal soup in which they swim.

Jurisdiction over patients lacking capacity

Some of the most legally difficult, emotionally agonizing, and politically explosive decisions in medical law involve the court making decisions on behalf of those who cannot make decisions for themselves—for instance children and permanently or temporarily incapacitous adults. Judges regularly order the compulsory sterilization of the mentally incompetent, permit doctors to tie a struggling Jehovah's Witness child to a table and give her the life-saving blood transfusion that her parents think will cause her to be hurled into the lake of fire for eternity, and tell doctors to withdraw artificial nutrition and hydration from unconscious patients (often over the protestations of the patients' families), so killing them.

Treatment decision cases are extreme, dramatic examples of a benevolently paternalistic jurisdiction with which everyone's familiar. Every day, all over the world, thousands of judges in family courts decide whether it will be best for a child to live with his mother or father. The same or similar judges, applying the same or similar criteria, decide whether it is better for the child to live or die. Judges regularly decide whether an incompetent adult's carer should be allowed to take money from the patient's account. To decide whether a doctor should be allowed to take her ovaries out of her pelvis is a very similar process.

A one-stop shop for resolving medical law disputes?

There is much wasteful duplication in medical litigation. If a doctor kills a patient by negligently clamping the wrong vessel during surgery, he might find himself, in respect of that single mistake, prosecuted for gross negligence manslaughter, pursued for damages by the patient's relatives and estate, watching his back at an inquest, and fighting for his registration before a regulatory tribunal. And that's not to mention other internal enquiries at the hospital, which might involve review of his employment contract. If he contends, as part of his defence, that the hospital was dangerously understaffed, it's perfectly possible that the issue of resource allocation might be discussed in one of the public law reviewing courts.

This multiplicity of proceedings makes no one but the lawyers happy. The doctor might have to give identical evidence five or six times, the relatives will have to hear the same distressing story over and over again (putting their grieving on hold until the lawyers have picked the case clean), and many expensive independent experts might be commissioned to comment on the same set of facts. It's possible that different tribunals might come to wholly different conclusions. The judge in the civil proceedings might decide that there was no negligence at all and that the doctor is an exemplary surgeon, but the disciplinary panel that the doctor was grossly negligent and should never practise again.

Can't it all be done in one set of proceedings, depriving the lawyers of their brief fees, the doctor of his stress, and the relatives of their distress?

The answer is no. Although they start with the same set of clinical facts, each of these types of proceedings has its own distinct objectives and corresponding procedures. They are not always compatible with the objectives and procedures of the others. The criminal proceedings, for instance, use a different definition of negligence from the civil proceedings, and have a higher standard of proof. The assessment of damages in the civil claim is a sophisticated process involving evidence about matters that are wholly irrelevant to any of the other jurisdictions. The inquest, concerned to learn lessons that will prevent the repetition of the tragedy, will inquire much more broadly into the background of the case than will the other tribunals.

That's not to say that something can't be done. Some European jurisdictions run criminal and compensatory inquiries to some extent along the same channel. We can learn from them. But, sadly, so long as we acknowledge that all the various objectives are legitimate, most of the lawyers will continue to be paid.

Chapter 3
Before birth

Despite its invasion by ultrasound and, sometimes, more dangerous tools, the uterus is a secret place. What happens there is biologically mysterious. The effects of gestation can be described in a fairly crude anatomical way. So too can a few of their more superficial causes. But the nature of the process and the detailed blueprint of the engine that drives it remain baffling.

The law has been content to leave metaphysics out of its own intrauterine fumblings. It has refused to be drawn into philosophical debate about the status of the early embryo, preferring to navigate the shadowlands of the unborn using its familiar instruments of rights and duties. It uses them with a fitting, deferential caution.

Rights and obligations to reproduce

The position in most places is this: if you want to be a parent, then generally, if nature's left you the option, you can be. You can fuse your gametes with almost anybody's. And if you don't want to be a parent, then you needn't be.

It's not surprising that the law defends the right to reproduce—or, at least, doesn't put many obstacles in the way of people wanting to do so. The urge to parenthood is one of the most fundamental urges there is, and the shadow of eugenics remains rightly scary.

Limitations on the right to reproduce are few and far between. Many cultures have, for obvious genetic reasons, prohibitions on incestuous unions, and, for the same genetic reasons, prohibit the creation of embryos by artificial reproductive procedures from the gametes of (for instance) parents and children, or siblings. Nor may you, in most places, create (or create and bring to term) a chimaeric embryo resulting from the fusion of human and non-human gametes. The state regulates reproduction by the young, too, by insisting that one cannot lawfully have sexual intercourse or marry below a certain age. But, incest, age, and technological bestiality aside, you can go forth and multiply.

Article 12 of the European Convention on Human Rights summarizes the international *zeitgeist*: 'Men and women of marriageable age have the right to marry and to found a family, according to the national laws governing the exercise of this right.' The second clause could drain the first of its significance, but in fact in no jurisdiction does it do so.

It doesn't follow, though, that you've got a right to state funding for in-vitro fertilization (IVF), or, if you've been locked up, that you can force the authorities to let your wife into jail for a conjugal visit at the time of your choice (see *ELH and PBH v United Kingdom* (1998-))- although if she's teetering on the edge of infertility it might be different: see *R (Mellor) v Secretary of State for the Home Department* (2002).

While it might be unsurprising to hear that there's a right to reproduce, it's so utterly unsurprising that there's no *obligation* to reproduce that it might seem odd to mention it at all. In fact there's a perfectly sensible reason for mentioning it—a reason that has been much discussed in the courts.

Before Diane Blood's husband died, some of his semen was harvested. Diane Blood wanted to use it to conceive a child. No, said the court. The rules prohibiting this were entirely reasonable: they were made to avoid the spectre of a man being confronted, emotionally or financially, by a child of whom he had no knowledge. The rule had a brutal consequence in that case, but that was no reason to overturn it: see *R v Human Fertilisation and Embryology Authority ex p Blood* (1997).

One might have thought that the situation would be different if it involved the implantation of already existing embryos, rather than the mere use of sperm. Perhaps the weight of the embryo's interest, joined to that of the mother's desire, would prevail over a man's reluctance to propagate. But no, the autonomistic right not to be a father trumps all the countervailing considerations: see *Evans v United Kingdom* (2006).

We see the same thinking at work where the father of an embryo asks the court to prevent his wife or girlfriend from having an abortion. Where abortion is lawful these applications have failed. The right not to be a parent outweighs the right to be one: see *Planned Parenthood of Central Missouri v Danforth* (1976); *C v S* (1988) and *Paton v United Kingdom* (1981).

From all this one might conclude that the rights of embryos and fetuses don't amount to much—at least where they conflict with almost any other rights. As a general proposition that's not inaccurate.

The rights and non-rights of the embryo and fetus

The law can't be accused of inflexible consistency. And still less of philosophical sophistication. At the time of writing, abortion was permitted in some circumstances in all countries in the world except for a very few, very Catholic Latin American countries. But those circumstances vary very widely. Some permit abortion only where it is necessary to save the woman's life; others permit it under any circumstances. Generally, and unsurprisingly, the more religiously committed the country, the harder it will be to have a lawful abortion. But that doesn't necessarily mean that countries with liberal abortion laws are blithe about the status of the embryo. On the contrary, their jurisprudential rhetoric often indicates a thoughtfulness sometimes lacking in the more stridently anti-abortion states. It's just (they'd say) that, having considered the matter carefully and painfully, they've decided that the plainly identifiable rights of a solid, adult mother should prevail over the misty, conditional rights (if any) of the mysterious embryo.

This is nonsense, say the anti-abortion activists. Yes, you've got two sets of rights in competition here: those of the mother, and those of the embryo. Only very rarely will the mother's right to live be at stake. When it is, even the most conservative Catholic agrees that it's a different matter.

What's usually at stake is the mother's right to avoid an uncomfortable few months of inhabitation by a growing parasite, and then some truncation of her ability to live her life in exactly the way that she chooses. These, say the pro-lifers, are essentially convenience rights—the sort of rights protected, for instance, by Article 8 of the European Convention on Human Rights. And, goes the argument, they must always be trumped by the hugely more weighty right to life (expressed, for instance, in Article 2 of the Convention) possessed by the fetus. Isn't this obvious? Convenience rights must, logically, be conditional on and subservient to the right to live: if you don't live, you can't experience convenience.

Much has been said about this argument. We return to it in a moment. But for now it's enough to say that it has been thought to have enough force for legal writers and judges (many of whom want to keep open the option of legal abortion) to be wary of according any rights at all to the embryo—at least in its early stages. That's often taken the form of denying to the embryo/ fetus/unborn child (and what a storm erupts whenever one uses the term 'unborn child' incautiously) any legal personality at all. In such a scheme a child magically becomes a fully human being, invested with all the protection of the law, when (and essentially because) it moves the few inches from inside the uterus to outside the vagina. That has the advantage of neatness, but the disadvantage of discordance both with biological facts (the facts, for instance, of incremental fetal sophistication and the possibility of viability from about 23 weeks gestation) and with intuition.

In some areas of the law, though, it's legally convenient for the fetus to exist. And so, for those purposes, it does. In English law, for instance, a fetus can inherit an estate. But for other purposes it is not so convenient. And so, by legal sleight of hand, it vanishes. Now you see it, now you don't.

Here's how it's put:

> 'It is established beyond doubt for the criminal law, as for the civil law…that the child *en ventre sa mere* does not have a distinct human personality, whose extinguishment gives rise to any penalties or liabilities at common law.' *Attorney General's Reference (No. 3 of 1994)* (1998): UK House of Lords

> 'To permit an unborn child to sue its pregnant mother-to-be would introduce a radically new conception into the law; the unborn child and its mother as separate juristic persons in a mutually separable and antagonistic relation…' *Winnipeg Child and Family Services (Northwest Area) v G* (1997): Canada, Supreme Court

> 'There can be no doubt that in England and Wales the foetus has no right of action, no right at all, until birth.' *Paton v Trustees of the British Pregnancy Advisory Services* (1979): UK, Court of Appeal

The device of the inconsistently existing fetus has been used for various purposes. In Canada and in many other places, for instance, a fetus cannot sue its mother for causing it damage during pregnancy. And yet if a doctor, or anyone else, causes the fetus harm (for example by negligently administering drugs to a pregnant mother), the fetus, once born, can sue the doctor for damages. The doctor couldn't say: 'At the time of my negligence you didn't exist: how can I possibly have injured a non-existent person?' or 'Your identity was inextricable from that of your mother, and so she should be suing, not you.'

There's a glaring anomaly here. What the law is really doing is saying to the fetus: 'If you survive gestation and become a person, we will retrospectively credit you with sufficient personality to be legally injured.' That's intellectually uncomfortable. So too is the mother's immunity—particularly if retrospective credit is really what's going on. Why should the person who is most obviously connected to the child, who has the greatest ability to harm and protect it, who should (surely) be regarded as having some sort of trusteeship responsibility to the unborn child, be the only person incapable of being fixed with meaningful legal responsibility?

At other times it's useful for the embryo/fetus/unborn child to exist *in some sense*. And so, it's now unsurprising to hear, it does. It is given sufficient existence and the necessary qualities for the purpose in hand.

Some examples. In IVF procedures, many 'spare' embryos are produced. How should they be treated? Intuition suggests that they should be treated with respect, and so they are given sufficient status to justify that respect. Most jurisdictions have legislation or case law that says more or less that. The UK Polkinghorne Committee on the use of embryos/fetuses in research (1989) expressed the international consensus. It spoke of the fetus having 'a special status...at every stage of its development which we wish to characterize as a profound respect based on its potential to develop into a fully formed human being'.

In the context of forced treatment of a pregnant mother, in order to save the child, the English Court of Appeal observed that 'Whatever else it may be, a 36-week foetus is not nothing; if viable, it is not lifeless, and it is certainly human': *St George's NHS Trust v S* (1998).

This convenient but slightly disreputable agnosticism about the legal status of the embryo/fetus is the current position of the European Court of Human Rights. That position emerged out of the tragic events in Lyons General Hospital.

Two women, both called Mrs Vo, were there on the same day. One was six months pregnant. The other was there to have a contraceptive coil removed. There was a mix-up. The doctors tried to remove the non-existent coil from the pregnant Mrs Vo, puncturing her amniotic sac. The pregnancy was doomed. A termination was performed.

The case found its way to Strasbourg. The question was whether the unborn child had a right to life under Article 2 of the European Convention on Human Rights. The relevant part of the Article states: 'Everyone's right to life shall be protected by law.' But did 'everyone' include an unborn child? The consequences of an unqualified 'yes' were of course profound. Abortion laws would be in jeopardy.

So the majority opted for equivocation. It decided not to decide, observing that 'at European level...there is no consensus on the nature and status of the embryo and/or fetus...At best, it may be regarded as common ground between States that the embryo/ fetus belongs to the human race. The potentiality of that being and its capacity to become a person—enjoying protection under the civil law...require protection in the name of human dignity, without making it a "person" with the "right to life" for the purposes of Article 2...Having regard to the foregoing, the Court is convinced that it is neither desirable, nor even possible as matters stand, to answer in the abstract the question whether the unborn child is a person for the purposes of Article 2' (*Vo v France* (2004)). So: it has some status, but we're not going to tell you what that status is, or its corollaries.

The position in the US is very similar. The fetus isn't a 'person' within the meaning of the 14th Amendment of the Federal Constitution (see, for instance, Blackmun J in *Roe v Wade* (1973)) and yet in some circumstances (and particularly once it reaches the crucial watershed of about three months' gestation) may nonetheless, by analogy, or by legal wriggle, or by political expediency, be entitled to 14th Amendment protection.

So it is that the law has been able to limp by with piecemeal solutions. Without a clearly identifiable status, it's going to be hard for embryos to resist harm. They will be outgunned by just about any real person. And even unreal people. One of the objections to granting embryos rights in the same currency as the rights of real people is that embryos are only potential people. And yet research on embryos is often permitted (for instance in the UK) on the grounds that the research may be of value to people as yet unborn. I'm not saying that's wrong; but it is untidy.

The state rarely insists that a mother must not carry a child to term, although it insists that children of a particular genetic complexion should not be conceived in the first place (the laws against incest). But it may happen. An incapacitous patient who becomes pregnant may be forced, against her will, to have an abortion. The judgment will typically be expressed in the language of the best interests both of the mother and of the welfare (were it to be born) of the child. What's happening here?

The maternal best interests part of the analysis is fairly straightforward. This isn't really an abortion against the mother's will. She's got no (rightly directed) will. But what about the interests of the putative child? A couple of points. First: it is given a voice in the debate (although for other purposes it has no legal existence) because it is convenient for it to have it. It will obligingly deliver a speech saying that it doesn't want to exist, and will then shut up. It's allowed no other speech. Second: in the law of the UK and in many other jurisdictions a child cannot bring a claim based on the assertion 'It were better that my mother had not borne me.' It's regarded as offensive to public policy: see, for instance, *McKay v Essex AHA* (1982). If public policy forbids such a claim by a child, why should it permit it-still less invite it and rely on it-from an unborn child?

There's widespread public unease, and some judicial unease, about claims by parents in relation to the financial costs of unwanted children. These typically occur where a sterilization has been performed negligently, or there's been a failure to warn about the risk of a sterilization operation reversing. The parents then claim the costs of upkeep.

These are uncomfortable claims. They involve the parents unwishing the child. In the UK, the discomfort spread to the House of Lords, which said that the birth of a child should conclusively be presumed to be a blessing which more than cancelled out the associated financial detriment: see *McFarlane v Tayside Health Board* (2000). That's policy speaking. But it's a policy that doesn't seem to extend to regarding the unborn child as a blessing. Fair enough: who said that the law had to be internally consistent? Which brings us back to abortion itself.

There are two legal ways of looking at abortion. The first is expressed in terms of rights. One jurisdiction might say—perhaps at a particular time of gestation—that 'Abortion is a mother's right' or 'The fetus has a right not to be killed.' The second is that abortion is a prima facie wrong, but that there are defences to it. The first of these approaches is exemplified by the US, and the famous Supreme Court decision of *Roe v Wade* (1973). The second is exemplified by the UK.

The majority in *Roe* discovered, in the 14th Amendment's concept of personal liberty and restriction on state action, a constitutional protection of 'a woman's decision whether or not to terminate her pregnancy'. But the woman's right, said the court, was not absolute: a state, according to the majority, 'may properly assert important interests in safeguarding health, in maintaining medical standards, and in protecting potential life. At some point in pregnancy, these respective interests become sufficiently compelling to sustain regulation of the factors that govern the abortion decision.'

The state, then, legitimately acts as a referee in a struggle between two competing rights—those of the mother and those of the fetus. The fetus's rights grow incrementally. During the first trimester the state's primary interest is in protecting maternal rights. During this period 'the attending physician, in consultation with his patient, is free to determine, without regulation by the State, that in his medical judgement, the patient's pregnancy should be terminated'. But the state also has an interest in protecting fetal life. When might that justify interference with the woman's continuing right to determine what happens to her own body? The tipping point, held the court, was fetal viability. Then the fetus could have a 'meaningful life', independent of its mother.

Accordingly: in the first trimester, the state must leave the woman to choose. Thereafter, until fetal viability, the state may regulate abortion in ways that are reasonably related to the mother's health (which was clarified in *Doe v Bolton* (1973) to be determined as a medical judgement in the light of all the factors pertinent to maternal well-being). After the time of fetal viability the state may, if it chooses, regulate abortion, even to the point of banning it (except where abortion is necessary to preserve the mother's life or health).

There's an odd asymmetry here. The state is required to leave the mother alone in the first trimester. Put another way, it is required not to protect the fetus then. But it is not required (although it is permitted) to protect the fetus during the time of viability. Its two obligations (to protect maternal health and fetal life) are not equally onerous.

Many jurisdictions analyse abortion problems in a similar rights-based way. Often, in such analyses, the fetus is better protected than it is in the US. Many of the countries which assert that the right of the fetus to live should trump that of the mother to be uninhabited rest that assertion on theological presumptions about the status of the embryo (many Catholic and Islamic countries) or on some dignity-based beliefs about its status (for instance Germany).

The UK, in common with many of the Australian states, does not speak of abortion as a 'right' (although no doubt a contention along those lines could be advanced in the language of Article 8 of the European Convention on Human Rights which, very broadly, gives a right to live our lives as we please—which might include a right not to be encumbered with an unwanted child). It chooses instead to say that abortion is unlawful, except where it isn't. The fact is, though, that until 24 weeks of gestation (when the rules change) there is abortion on demand in the UK. That's not to say that there's a right to it: it's just to say that you won't have any difficulty finding a clinic to do your abortion for you in a way that will leave it entirely immune to prosecution.

This, ironically, makes life more dangerous for the fetus than in rights-based jurisdictions. Where the notion of rights is taken sufficiently seriously to be the basis of the mother's security, there's at least the possibility (theoretical though it often is) of the fetus putting up its developing arm and demanding, by the same token, a right to be heard.

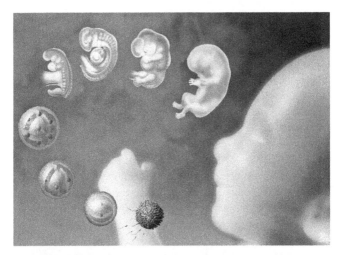

2. The developing embryo/fetus. Some contend that the moral and/or legal status of the embryo or fetus changes as it develops

The cloning debate

Identical twins are clones. They're not especially frightening or necessarily dysfunctional. And yet the spectre of creating clones is scary to almost everyone.

In relation to reproductive cloning (the cloning of an embryo with the intention of bringing it to term) the fears don't seem to be located consistently in respect for the status of the human embryo. Instead they are fears about overstepping the limits of legitimate interference with nature ('playing God'), or distaste at the thought of a woman giving birth to herself or her partner, with all the psychological fallout that would entail for everyone involved.

The ethics are complicated. The law, by and large, is not. Human reproductive cloning is unlawful almost everywhere. The regulation of therapeutic cloning (the creation of cloned embryos with the intention of using them for research) is more politically controversial. It is permitted in the UK, for instance, with decisions about the permissibility of a particular application being delegated to an independent scrutineer (the Human Fertilisation and Embryology Authority). In the US, regulation is a patchwork of state and federal legislation. When a Republican government is in, embryo research will tend to be out.

Where embryo research is unlawful, the legislature has made some sort of judgment about the status of the embryo, and decided that the respect the embryo deserves warrants the disadvantage to potential beneficiaries of research that prohibition of research will entail—some sort of calculus along the lines of: 'The moral bad involved in the creation of embryos and their destruction outweighs the moral good of a chance of curing motor neurone disease.' That sort of calculus is easy enough if the potential good is to unidentified people. It's easy to dismiss a faceless abstraction. It's much harder to look a real person in the eye and say: 'For my belief in the inviolability of the eight-cell embryo you must die.' That's often what the 'saviour sibling' cases boil down to.

Saviour siblings

Zain Hashmi, aged three, had beta-thallasaemia. His best chance of survival was by receiving stem cells from the umbilical cord of a sufficiently well tissue-matched sibling.

The chances of conceiving such a sibling naturally were not good. So his parents sought permission to create embryos by IVF. Then, at about the eight-cell stage, a cell would be taken from each embryo and tested to see if the embryo would do the job. The application was approved by the UK regulatory body, but a pro-life group, opposed both to the destruction of the unused embryos and to what they saw as the instrumentalizing of human life, challenged the approval. It lost: see *Quintavalle (on behalf of*

Comment on Reproductive Ethics) v Human Fertilisation and Embryology Authority (2005). The case turned on some technical niceties, but the point of principle remained painfully clear. It divided even the pro-life lobby. Are you really pro-life if you're content for a three-year-old to die?

Similar cases have made judges in several jurisdictions pace the floorboards in the early hours. Lawyers tend to like absolute positions: to say that something has a definite, inalienable status. They tend to think that such positions make life easier. But if everything with a human genome has inalienable human status, the most religious, conservative judges are forced into a moral and legal relativism that is visibly uncomfortable for them. Life's not straightforward if you abandon your stereotypes and see it as it really is. And since life isn't straightforward, nor can the law be.

Chapter 4
Confidentiality and privacy

Patients tell doctors intimate things. At least since about 500 BC, when the Hippocratic Oath required doctors to declare that 'Whatsover I shall see or hear in the course of my profession...if it be what should not be published abroad, I will never divulge, holding such things to be holy secrets,' everyone has agreed that there are some times when doctors shouldn't disclose them. Most agree that only rarely should doctors disclose any of their patients' confidences. But should there be an absolute rule of non-disclosure? If not, why not? When is disclosure justified? Is disclosure ever mandatory? These questions have made lots of normally prosaic judges express themselves in unusually philosophical language.

National and international codes of medical ethics acknowledge, in their equivocation, the undesirability of an absolute rule. That equivocation is there in Hippocrates. He seems to recognize that there may be some things that can ethically be 'published abroad'. One of the American Medical Association's 'Principles of Medical Ethics' is: 'A physician shall...safeguard patient confidences within the constraints of the law'—so handing the really difficult questions to the lawyers. The World Medical Association's International Code of Medical Ethics, revised in 2006, is more helpful. It anticipates some of the caveats the law has found necessary. 'A physician shall respect a patient's right to confidentiality. It is ethical to disclose confidential information when the patient consents to it or when there is a real and imminent threat of harm to the patient or to others and this threat can be only removed by a breach of confidentiality.' The UK General Medical Council tells doctors that '[p]atients have a right to expect that information about them will be held in confidence by their doctors. You must treat information about patients as confidential, including after a patient has died,' but peppers that principle liberally with caveats in a mass of detailed supplementary advice. Other health-care professionals have similar guidelines.

Why should confidences be respected?

Many reasons have been identified by the courts. Some are utilitarian. It's typically said, for instance, that a law of medical confidentiality facilitates the flow of information from patients to doctors. If patients think that their secrets will be the stuff of gossip in the hospital canteen, they will be less likely to tell the doctor the full story. That's not good either for the patient or for the doctor: it reduces the chance of the patient getting the treatment he needs. The point doesn't apply just to that particular doctor and that particular patient: it applies more broadly to the medical profession. If doctors as a whole aren't bound by a duty of confidentiality, patients *generally* will be less forthcoming, and the general confidence that the public reposes in the medical profession will be reduced.

Some reasons for keeping tight-lipped are more fundamental. Patients, it is commonly said, have a *right* to secrecy.

Confidential to whom?

Of course it's important for treating clinicians to talk intelligently to one another about patient care. Both law and ethics are pragmatic about this. The pragmatism is based on an assumption about what patients expect. If a confidence is divulged to doctor X, X will be entitled to tell it to doctor Y, as long as the disclosure is necessary for the proper care of the patient. Why? Because the patient will be taken to expect this disclosure, and therefore impliedly to have consented to it.

But there are limits to this implied consent, and those limits are often exceeded. Patients at a teaching hospital no doubt expect their medical secrets to be discussed with medical students, but does a woman going to her family doctor for an abortion referral really know that the referral letter will be typed by the receptionist, who probably lives round the corner and will bump into her at the supermarket?

From ethics to law

Several different types of language have been used to translate these ethical positions into legal principles.

Some analyses see the patient's secrets as a sort of intellectual property which is handed to the doctor on the strict understanding that the property will only be used for the purposes for which it is being given. The doctor is a sort of bailor or trustee. To deal with the secrets other than in the authorized way is a breach of the trust: it's like using a borrowed car for joyriding. Or it's a breach of an express or implied contract with the doctor, by which the doctor agrees that his lips will be sealed. Which brings us to another way of looking at the issue: the doctor's conscience. Decent doctors, with properly oriented consciences, don't go metaphorically joyriding, or break their promises. A British Court of Appeal judge, Simon Brown LJ, having reviewed a number of authorities, concluded that:

> To my mind the one clear and consistent theme emerging... is this: the confidant is placed under a duty of good faith to the confider and the touchstone by which to judge the scope of his duty and

whether or not it has been fulfilled or breached is his own conscience, no more and no less... (*R v Department of Health, ex p Source Informatics Ltd* (2000))

Trustee- and conscience-based analyses feed happily into the notion of duty. Indeed much of the law of confidentiality has been forged in the crucible of tort litigation for damages for breach of confidence, where, of course, the notion of duty is so at home.

Some of these models clunk. Today, in many jurisdictions, they are being eclipsed by human rights analyses. The European Convention on Human Rights is one good example. Article 8(1) of the Convention provides that '[e]veryone has the right to respect for his private and family life, his home and his correspondence'. This is the most elastic of all the Convention articles. It has been found to stretch to areas of the law undreamt of by the draftsman, and it certainly extends to the medical consultation room. It makes patient autonomy the starting point. And often the end point. 'The protection of personal data,' said the European Court of Human Rights in *Z v Finland* (1998), 'not least medical data, is of fundamental importance to a person's enjoyment of his or her right to respect for private and family life as guaranteed by Article 8 of the Convention.' Quite right.

Although the language of human rights is rather different from that of contract, trusteeship, and duty, there's hardly a difference in substance. Just as dutiful doctors don't normally breach contracts, dutiful doctors don't normally breach their patients' human rights. The UK House of Lords, in *Campbell v MGN* (2004), suggested that the test to apply in deciding whether or not a claim for breach of confidence gets off the ground is whether the claimant had a 'reasonable expectation of privacy'. That neatly conflates the demands of the common law and the Convention. The European Convention has changed the way that lawyers frame their medical confidentiality claims: it hasn't, by and large, changed the outcome of those claims.

Privacy and confidentiality are closely related and, in most countries, creeping gradually closer. The UK judges, for instance, nervous about being over-creative, insist that there is no tort of the invasion of privacy per se, but that there is a tort of misuse of private information. There's nothing wrong, then, with a press photographer taking a salacious photo of a celebrity, but if he does anything at all with it the law gets stern. In most real medical contexts confidentiality and the embryonic law of privacy can be safely regarded as identical.

Take, for instance, the whiteboards that appear in many hospitals above the nurses' station. They often identify the patient and her date of birth, and may go on to indicate the condition for which she's in the hospital. The boards are visible to everyone when they come onto the ward. Is this a breach of privacy? Yes, although English lawyers would look troubled when they admit it. It's also a breach of confidentiality. At least in England, both the law of confidentiality and the tort of misuse of private information have the muscle to do something about it.

Balancing competing interests: the basic position

So far, easy enough. Confidences matter. There's no controversy about that. Their importance, and the corresponding obligations on doctors, can be described in many ways. But from now on the plot thickens. For patients are not islands: they are relational entities. They cannot coherently be considered except as part of the nexus of relationships in which they exist and of which, to a large extent, they consist.

Mr W was a very dangerous man. He was locked up in a secure hospital. He optimistically applied to be released. He asked a psychiatrist, Dr Egdell, to write a report saying how outrageous his continued incarceration was. Dr Egdell wasn't fooled, and instead wrote that W had a long-standing and morbid fascination with explosives, and would pose a serious risk if released.

W's solicitors' optimism faded, but their determination did not. They did not disclose the report to the tribunal. This worried Dr Egdell. Without W's permission, he disclosed his report. W was outraged. He sued Dr Egdell for damages for breach of confidence.

The case illustrates well the way that medical lawyers in most jurisdictions look at the law of confidentiality. There's a widely accepted checklist of core questions.

Was the information disclosed in circumstances of confidentiality? Of course. Almost all information disclosed in most normal medical circumstances will be. You can say, if you like, that a duty of confidentiality arose. It doesn't much matter how you describe that duty, but if you choose to use duty language you need to recognize that the duty to the patient is not an absolute one. It is hedged round with phrases like '...except where...' Does this mean that the physician has a competing duty to someone else? Well, possibly. We'll come to that.

Was there disclosure? Plainly, yes. It might have been different if the information was already in the public domain. A well-recognized defence to the allegation of letting cats out of bags is that the cat is already out of the bag and on the front page of a newspaper.

Was that the end of the matter? Did W therefore succeed? No. He failed. The crucial question, the court decided, was whether the public interest in disclosure outweighed the *public* interest in non-disclosure. The italics are important. The relevant interest in maintaining the confidence was not W's: it wasn't like a property right. The court implicitly endorsed the utilitarian reasons for keeping confidences. Here, there was a public interest in major buildings staying upright and shoppers staying alive. That interest outweighed the utilitarian considerations that apply to this and all other medical confidence cases: see *W v Egdell* (1990).

Nowadays, if Dr Egdell were acting on behalf of a public authority, the arguments would be framed additionally in terms of Article 8. A similar balancing exercise would be done. Was there a prima facie breach of W's Article 8(1) right? Certainly. But Article 8 has two parts. 8(2) provides that: 'There shall be no interference by a public authority with the exercise of [the right in 8(1)] except such as is in accordance with the law and is necessary in a democratic society in the interests of national security, public safety or the economic well-being of the country, for the prevention of disorder or crime, for the protection of health or morals, or for the protection of the rights and freedoms of others.' An interference with W's right could plainly be justified on all or any of the grounds identified in 8(2).

Where the duty of confidentiality *must* be breached

Very broadly, courts across the world have approached problems of confidentiality like this. And legislatures and courts worldwide have indicated that there are some cases in which the doctor must disclose information given to him in confidence. These cases are best seen as determinations that the public interest in disclosure is so overwhelming that no other considerations could possibly prevail against it.

Doctors must disclose information when a court says they must. If they don't, they will be in contempt of court, and can be locked up. It is obviously in the public interest that the truth emerges in legal proceedings. But what if the truth can only emerge by breaching patient confidentiality?

In England, there is no blanket rule of doctor–patient privilege, entitling or requiring a doctor to keep quiet. But in both civil and criminal proceedings the fact that patient confidentiality will be breached by an answer to a question or the production of a document is a factor that the court can consider in deciding whether or not to require that answer or that document. The court conducts the now familiar exercise, balancing the public interest in disclosure against that in non-disclosure. It often expresses itself in terms of proportionality.

In the US, most states have rules of evidence that give patients some patchy, conditional protection against disclosure by their doctors. These rules tend to be particularly keen on sealing the lips of psychotherapists. The Federal Rules of Evidence contain no such privilege, although the Supreme Court's respect for the sanctity of the modern confessional—the shrink's couch—has created an arguable but fragile privilege in relation to disclosure by psychotherapists: see *Jaffee v Redmond* 518 US 1 (1996).

As one would expect, jurisdictions come to illuminatingly different conclusions about what type of disclosure is perceived to be in the public interest. But there are some common elements. It is generally thought to be good for societies to know more or less who lives among them (hence rules for the mandatory disclosure of the medical facts of births and deaths), for their members not to be struck down by contagious diseases (hence public health laws requiring doctors to expose the otherwise private fact that a patient is suffering from a notifiable disease), and to be protected from terrorism (hence, in many places, such as the UK, a requirement to hand over information about terrorists, even if that information is contained in medical records or disclosed in the course of an otherwise confidential consultation).

Outside these fairly clear (and usually statutory) cases, the position is much more ethically fuzzy and legally difficult.

Suppose that a patient tells his psychiatrist that he is going to kill his wife. The psychiatrist believes him, but tells no one what he has been told, thinking that it would be an unpardonable breach of medical confidentiality to do so. The patient bludgeons his wife to death. Can the wife's family successfully sue the doctor? What they would be saying is: 'You had a duty to breach the patient's medical confidentiality. That duty to breach was a duty owed to his wife.'

Several jurisdictions have smiled on that contention—for instance California (*Tarasoff v The Regents of the University of California* (1976)) and England (*Palmer v South Tees Health Authority* (1999)). Those were claims in tort. Tort is concerned with the question of whether the defendant, X, owes a duty to the claimant, Y. It is understandably reluctant to impose on X a duty to the whole world, and restricts the ambit of duties using the devices of proximity, foreseeability, and reasonableness.

What would the law of tort say, then, about the liability of a psychiatrist who failed to disclose not a specific threat to the wife, but a conclusion that the patient was generally dangerous to unspecified people? If one of the unspecified people got very specifically stabbed in the throat, would he be able to sue the psychiatrist, saying, as the dead wife did in the first example: 'You had a duty to me to breach the patient's confidentiality'?

The law of tort would be more queasy about this submission, but should that queasiness determine what, as a matter of public policy, the law should say about the psychiatrist's obligation to disclose? The questions of public good that govern the general law of confidentiality don't fit neatly in the private law world of tort claims, but it would be little comfort to the stabbing victim to say: It's important that public and private law are concordant and, I'm afraid, private law trumps public. You've no claim.' Shouldn't ethics, rather than artificial legal theory, cut the Gordian knot? Shouldn't one ask simply: 'Is it so obviously right to blow the whistle on the patient that the psychiatrist cannot be excused for not blowing it?'

In most jurisdictions the law sees the force of this question but, in almost all cases, has refused to agree that it is so obviously right to disclose that the doctor *must*, and has contented itself with saying, in most conscience-troubling instances, that the doctor *can* disclose without sanction. It will very often be, therefore, that a doctor will not be condemned by the law either for disclosing or for not disclosing.

The law has often, and rightly, taken its cue from the professional regulatory organizations that are deemed to be the conscience of the profession. If, for instance, the UK General Medical Council says that disclosure in particular circumstances is mandatory, then the law will agree, and conscientious obligation becomes crystallized into law. That there are so few examples of mandatory disclosure is a mark of the professions' own reluctance to legislate for every conceivable set of facts.

Where the duty of confidentiality *may* be breached

There are two points here. The first is that there's an ethos of judicial liberality—of sympathy with the awful dilemmas that face the doctor at the clinical coalface. The second is rather more black-letter.

First: judicial sympathy. The medico-legal landscape is composed mostly of no-man's-land, stretched messily between bordering principles, and pockmarked by the craters made by litigious shells. The law of confidentiality is the classic example. In most real cases, lawyers and health-care professionals have to navigate their own way through this mess, guided by more or less bad analogies with decided cases, by the guidelines given by their professional organizations, and by the compass of their own conscience.

The law says that a breach of confidence is not actionable if the public interest in the disclosure outweighs the public interest in non-disclosure. That's often a very difficult balancing exercise. In practice it is delegated to individual clinicians: you can't litigate every problem that involves a question of confidentiality. Clinicians have to undertake the exercise without the (theoretical) benefit of detailed arguments from counsel, or the (actual) benefit of ample time for reflection. And so it is not surprising that the courts judge clinicians' judgements kindly. The doctor disclosed? Fine: we can understand why. The doctor didn't disclose? Fine: we can understand why.

Second: the black-letter law of lawful but not mandatory disclosure.

The starting point for the lawyers is set by the professional organizations. The law is rarely stricter on the profession than is the profession itself, and is often more lenient. The bigger the professional organization, though, the more unhelpfully general the guideline. The World Medical Association, for example, suggests that a doctor may disclose secrets if 'a real and imminent threat of harm to the patient or to others' may be averted only by a breach of confidentiality. That puts the test too liberally for most jurisdictions. Does a remote risk of an infinitesimal harm to a third party justify disclosure? The WMA would seem to say that it did. Many other regulatory organizations have been more cautious. The UK General Medical Council indicates that disclosure without the patient's consent may be appropriate where failure to disclose 'may expose others to a risk of death or serious harm... You should still seek the patient's consent to disclosure if practicable and consider any reasons given for refusal... Such a situation might arise, for example, when a disclosure would be likely to assist in the prevention, detection or prosecution of serious crime, especially crimes against the person.' The American Medical Association advises that 'When a patient threatens to inflict serious physical harm to another person or to him or herself and there is a reasonable probability that the patient may carry out the threat, the physician should take reasonable precautions for the protection of the intended victim, which may include notification of law enforcement authorities.'

How might these issues arise in practice? Well, a doctor might feel obliged to turn in a predatory would-be axe murderer. But even today, this is not part of most doctors' daily diet. Much more common is the risk posed by infectious disease.

A businessman comes into a doctor's surgery and confesses that on a recent trip to Thailand he had unprotected sexual intercourse with a prostitute. He is concerned that he might have contracted HIV. He's right to be worried. He has. The doctor questions him about his wife. She doesn't know, says the patient, and she's not going to know. And, what's more, he's not going to stop having sex with her, and he's not going to use a condom.

What should the doctor do?

In most jurisdictions the doctor can, entirely safely, tell the wife that she's at risk. Indeed the law is tending increasingly in the direction of insisting that he should. Tort will be more likely to

3. Sometimes clear breaches of medical confidentiality are justified because the public interest in disclosure outweighs the public (or private) interest in keeping the secret

condemn him for non-disclosure if the wife is his patient, but neither ethics nor the general law of confidentiality should mind whose life he endangers: it's a *public* interest in disclosure that's being considered. The wife is just the part of the public that's most directly in the viral firing line.

Children, incapacitous patients, and the secrets of the dead

The law of consent and the law of confidentiality are close relatives. Confidentiality is happy about disclosure when the patient consents, and uneasy about it when the patient does not. But there are some classes of patient who cannot give consent. Young children do not have the neurological software necessary to understand what's at stake in the disclosure or non-disclosure of their secrets. Capacity can be truncated by illness or injury. And the dead, so far as we know, have no opinions.

It's therefore no surprise that, in relation to children and incapacitous patients, the law of confidentiality trundles in the wake of the law of consent. That is so in all jurisdictions. The starting point in England, therefore, is accordingly the best interests of the patient. If disclosure is, prima facie, against the patient's best interests, there is a presumption against disclosure. But, as in the rest of the law of confidentiality, that's not the end of the story. The interests of others fall into the balance too, and are weighed in precisely the same way as for any other confidentiality case.

An area that gives particular trouble is the provision of contraceptive services to children. Suppose a 14-year-old girl comes to see a doctor. She wants to go on the contraceptive pill because she is having sex with her 14-year-old boyfriend. (It might be different if the boyfriend were 45: then the girl might have been giving the doctor information about a dangerous sexual predator, and other considerations might come into play.) Should the parents know what's going on? In England the court has said that it should be assumed that parental involvement will be helpful (which means that it is in the girl's best interests) (*R (Axon) v Secretary of State for Health* (2006)), but that this assumption can be displaced. The American Medical Association has given more or less identical advice: see Opinion 5.055: Confidential Care for Minors: 1996. It's easy to understand why the assumption of disclosure is readily displaced: girls would often be discouraged from seeking medical help if they thought that their parents would be told.

The dead, in many countries, can't be libelled, but, anomalously, their secrets may be protected. Professional organizations (for instance the GMC and the AMA) presume that medical secrets should be kept confidential after the patient's death, subject to the usual balancing exercise. It seems, though, that the interests of family members or friends in knowing the circumstances of a death will weigh heavily. While one might see this as acknowledging a public interest in the truth emerging and angst being dissipated, it seems rather artificial.

The law, while smiling broadly on these well-meaning expressions, has generally been content to sit on the fence. The English case of *Lewis v Secretary of State for Health* (2008) is typical. It held that it was *arguable* that the duty of confidentiality survived the grave.

Consent and confidentiality are close cousins. Let's visit the cousin.

Chapter 5
Consent

People tend to assume that they have an absolute right to control what is done with their bodies. But it's not so simple.

A group of homosexual sadomasochists met in private. Their idea of a good night out was to nail one another's genitalia to pieces of wood. They were all adults, and it was all consensual. No one complained, but the police got to hear of it. The participants were prosecuted for various assault offences. They simply said: 'Everyone consented. Consent is a defence to assault.' They were convicted by the English courts, and the convictions survived a trip to the European Court of Human Rights: see *R v Brown* (1994); *Laskey, Jaggard and Brown v UK* (1997).

The judges who upheld the convictions and those who would have quashed them all based their decisions on an appeal to public policy. No one thought that sadomasochism should be encouraged. Lord Templeman's attitude was typical: 'The evidence discloses that the practices of the appellants were unpredictably dangerous and degrading to body and mind...Society is entitled and bound to protect itself against a cult of violence...'

The judgments turned on the extent to which the state should be allowed to reach into the private lives of citizens. Some judges were more liberal than others, but it's as trite a proposition as one can get that the law restricts what individuals can do. Indeed one might even *define* the law as that which restricts individual freedom. Normally a curtailing of X's freedom is justified on the grounds that if X is not restricted, Y will be adversely affected in an unacceptable way. That adverse effect might be direct and physical (which is why, for instance, X's freedom to rape Y is curtailed by the criminal law), psychologically corrupting (which is why some forms of censorship of violent video games might be justified), or by an insidious transformation of ethos or atmosphere (which is one reason why legislation prohibiting assisted suicide, and so asserting the value of human life, might be justified, although it interferes with an individual's ability to end their life in the circumstances they wish).

Brown is sometimes cited as establishing that one cannot validly consent to serious bodily injury. The state, on this analysis, has a paternalistic duty to protect us from ourselves. But if that's right, it discharges its duty in a very inconsistent way. Boxers can injure themselves grievously for money, and crowds can roar enthusiastically as noses break and blood spurts. Skiing and bungee jumping are lawful, and when you get injured doing either you will get free medical treatment from the state in many countries. The state has a duty to prevent the suicide of an entirely mentally competent prisoner. And no one suggests that a surgeon acts unlawfully if he does wholly unnecessary breast augmentation or female genital cosmetic surgery—in the course of which he will inflict what amounts to (at least until the wounds heal) significant bodily injury.

The law of consent is so suffused with policy that it is sometimes difficult to map the outlines of the law. The policy itself is a creature of the tension between autonomy on the one hand and community interest and state ideology on the other.

That said, there are some generally recognized principles.

Competent adults

What's a competent adult?

Competency or capacity in relation to a particular decision is the ability to receive, weigh, process, and retain the relevant information. It also implies an ability to communicate the decision made once the information is processed. The words 'in relation to a particular decision' are crucial. Capacity is not an all-or-nothing thing. One might well have capacity for one decision but not for another. You don't need much neurological processing power to understand sufficiently what's involved in the dressing of your bedsore. You need much more to ponder the pros and cons of a cancer chemotherapy regime.

Capacity can fluctuate. If I drink 20 pints of beer, my ability to make decisions about my own medical treatment, or indeed about anything, will be seriously reduced. But in the morning it will be restored. Therapeutic drugs can have a similar effect. So can some diseases. Depression might impair my capacity: nature, TLC or Prozac might restore it.

Legal systems across the world rightly value autonomy, and fear terribly the thought of forcing unwanted treatment on a patient. They accordingly tend to require clinicians and others to presume that a patient is capacitous unless the contrary is proved, and to seek to ensure that, if at all possible, decisions are made by the patient herself, rather than by someone else on her behalf. It might follow, for instance, that if a decision about treatment can safely be delayed until a temporarily incapacitous patient regains capacity, there should be a delay.

Suppose a surgeon, while operating to break down pelvic adhesions, finds an ovarian tumour. It's not *immediately* life threatening, but the surgeon feels that it should be dealt with. Unless the woman wants to die, the tumour will have to come out some time. He removes the tumour. The patient, of course, has not given express consent. The surgeon justifies his action by saying that, since the patient is anaesthetized and thus incapacitous, he can and should do what is objectively in her best interests, or (depending on the jurisdiction) what she would want were she in a position to say.

The court would not be impressed. The patient's incapacity is temporary. She could have been woken up and her real wishes ascertained.

Competent adults: the general rule

At least within the walls of a hospital, a competent adult can generally consent to anything, and her refusal to consent to anything must be respected.

The classic statement of this principle comes from the US. Cardozo J in *Schloendorff v Society of New York Hospital* (1914):

> Every human being of adult years and sound mind has a right to determine what shall be done with his own body; and a surgeon who performs an operation without his patient's consent commits an assault, for which he is liable in damages.

And in Canada:

> The state's interest in preserving the life or health of a competent patient must generally give way to the patient's stronger interest in directing the course of her own life . . . The right to determine what shall be done with one's body is a fundamental right in our society. The concepts inherent in this right are the bedrock upon which the principles of self-determination and individual autonomy are based. Free individual choice in matters affecting this right should . . . be accorded very high priority. (*Malette v Shulman* (1990))

It doesn't matter that a choice might be deadly. Competent adult Jehovah's Witnesses can refuse life-saving blood transfusions. As long as you understand the consequences of what you're asking for, you can insist that the doctors switch off the ventilator which is breathing for you. The basic rule is: autonomy's respected to death.

This doesn't mean, of course, that you can require someone actively to do anything to you. Generally you can't demand that an individual doctor provides a particular treatment, or, in a publicly funded health system, that the state provides a particular treatment that no clinician believes is in your best interests. You can require someone to stop your life-sustaining ventilator because the continued ventilation is, without your consent, an inappropriate act—indeed an assault. So one can demand omissions (refuse treatment), but not demand acts (insist on specific treatment).

Incompetent adults

If a decision has to be made about (for instance) medical treatment, and someone can't make it for themselves, someone will have to make it for them. Making someone submit to medical treatment that they haven't themselves endorsed is philosophically draconian, and may be physically draconian. It might do more harm than good. One might have to get burly nurses to hold the patient down on a table until they are anaesthetized. That shouldn't be done lightly, and by and large isn't.

How does one decide how to make a decision on someone else's behalf, and who does it?

The 'who does it?' is more difficult to summarize than one might think. The real answer is either the patient themselves (where the patient has made a binding advance decision saying what they would like to happen should they become incapacitous), a proxy decision-maker appointed by the patient while they have the capacity to do so, or the court.

Part of the law's respect for autonomy is expressed in its respect for the wishes of a patient, recorded at a time when they were capacitous, regarding what they would like to happen if they lose their capacity. (Some of the difficulties with advance decisions are discussed in Chapter 9, on the end of life). If an advance decision has complied with any relevant formalities, was appropriately informed at the time it was made, applies to the relevant clinical circumstances, and if there is no indication that the patient might have decided differently were she to be able to make the decision himself as of now, the advance decision will be honoured, and quite right too. But there are many 'buts' here.

In many jurisdictions a person can appoint a proxy decision-maker. When they do, and the proxy is acting within the scope of the authority delegated to them, the proxy's decision is as valid as if it were uttered capacitously by the patient.

If there is no relevant advance decision and no validly exercised proxy, the court decides.

It might not always seem like that. Indeed it is actually very rare indeed for the court to be troubled with medical decision-making. Almost all decisions on behalf of patients are taken by the clinicians concerned or, in the case of non-medical decisions (such as where to live, where to bank, what to eat), by carers or family. What's really going on here?

What the doctors or carers are doing, if they're acting lawfully, is to act as the agents of the relevant national court, which itself is the custodian of the law. The court retains ultimate jurisdiction. A decision made on behalf of an incompetent patient by anyone can always be overruled by the court.

How, then, can the doctor or carer act lawfully? It depends on the particular jurisdiction concerned. If the patient is in the UK, for instance, the decision will be a lawful one if it is in the best interests of the patient. In many states in the US the test is, instead, that of substituted judgement: the decision-maker must divine what the

4. Tom, the subject of Hogarth's series *A Rake's Progress*, is finally incarcerated in 'Bedlam', a London psychiatric hospital. The law has long recognized that some mental states justify treatment to which the patient will not or cannot consent

patient would have done in the relevant circumstances had she capacity to make the decision. These tests are discussed in Chapter 9, in the context of end-of-life decision-making, where the questions present in the most dramatic form.

Children

Every jurisdiction has a formal definition of a 'child' for legal purposes. In the UK a 'child', for the purpose of medical decision-making, is anyone under the age of 18. The definitions sometimes create curious anomalies. A court might find a boy of 12 guilty of murder, but he's not entitled to refuse treatment for his own acne.

Very broadly, children do not have (or it is assumed that they do not have) the ability of competent adults to understand the consequences of their decisions. But this statement is too broad to be the sole basis of responsible law-making. It's plainly foolish to assume that as midnight strikes to usher in her 18th birthday, a child is suddenly given a completely new set of cognitive faculties. And many 17-year-olds (and 16-year-olds, and no doubt some eight-year-olds) will have a maturity and sophistication denied to many legally competent 50-year-olds. Nonetheless, lines have to be drawn somewhere.

The lines can work injustice. In most jurisdictions treatment can be given to non-consenting children which is deemed to be in their best interests. But compulsorily treating a perfectly comprehending, sophisticated 17-year-old is a terrible thing. And so, generally, the law has allowed the lines to bend. Thus in the UK, which is fairly typical, there's the notion of '*Gillick* competency' (see *Gillick v West Norfolk and Wisbech AHA* (1986)). A child has the capacity to consent to medical treatment when she 'achieves a sufficient understanding and intelligence to enable...her to understand fully what is proposed'. That includes, of course, the ability to understand the consequences of not being treated. Whether a particular child has that understanding and intelligence is a question of fact.

In many legal systems there's an asymmetry between the law relating to a child's ability to consent to treatment and to refuse treatment. In the UK, for instance, statute provides that a 16- or 17-year-old's consent to treatment is as valid as that of an adult. But the same does not apply to refusals of treatment. There the common law, *Gillick* rule applies.

At first blush this looks illogical. But in fact it makes sense. It reflects the law's presumption that clinicians are likely to suggest to a child only treatment that is in the child's best interests. Accordingly the court can say, in response to a 16- or 17-year-old's refusal: 'We've looked at the case carefully, and it's clear that doctor knows best. You'll have the treatment.'

The question of parental consent or refusal of consent is vexed. It's often said, even by lawyers, that parents (or, more accurately, those with parental responsibility) have a right to make treatment decisions on behalf of their children. Consent forms are printed and hospital protocols devised with that in mind. But it's not the full legal truth.

What's really happening is that the law presumes that parents (being, usually, uniquely concerned and knowledgeable about their children) will be the best arbiter of what is in the child's best interests. But that presumption can be displaced. The final decision in relation to a child's treatment always rests with the court.

Take a seven-year-old child in a family of Jehovah's Witnesses. The child is knocked down by a car. If the child does not have a blood transfusion he will die. The devout parents refuse to give their consent. In their view, the eternal consequences of receiving the blood will be more serious than the child's physical death.

This is the sort of consent case that often reaches the court. In almost all such circumstances the court overrules the parents— deciding that it is in the child's best interests to live. In the US, for instance, the court said:

> Parents may be free to become martyrs themselves, but it does not
> follow that they are free in identical circumstances to make martyrs
> of their children ... (*Prince v Massachusetts* (1944))

But the court does not overrule the parents blithely. It considers carefully the sad fact that a child who receives blood may be rejected by her parents and cold-shouldered by the community. That fact is factored into the best-interests equation. One can imagine extreme circumstances where a child, if she survives, would in any event have a seriously diminished quality of life. If one adds to this the burden of ostracism, one may be forced to the conclusion that it is not in the child's best interests to have the life-saving transfusion.

The best-interests test has a long chronological perspective. It looks far into the future.

Imagine, for instance, that child X has leukaemia. His only realistic chance of survival lies in receiving a bone-marrow donation from his eight-year old sister, Y. This will involve sticking a large needle into Y and aspirating marrow. Y refuses to agree to the procedure. She hates her brother because he has just stolen her teddy bear. In fact, of course, her refusal is legally irrelevant: she cannot validly either give or refuse consent. The teddy bear incident will just make the business of getting the marrow that much more traumatic than it would be with a compliant child.

The test of whether Y should be forced to donate the marrow is simply whether it is in Y's best interests.

Courts in such circumstances have typically found that donation is in Y's best interests, although the aspiration itself is clearly a medical detriment. It is in Y's interests that her brother lives. Not only will Y have the benefit of growing up with X (dubious though she might see that benefit to be, just at the moment), but she will be spared the stigma of being her brother's de facto executioner. One could hardly expect her parents' attitude to her to be unaffected by the fact that she could have saved her brother but failed to do so.

When is consent not consent?

In Victoria, Australia, a perverted doctor inserted an instrument into a woman's vagina. His motivation was purely sexual: there was no clinical indication. The woman consented because she thought it was diagnostically necessary.

The doctor was tried for sexual assault. He was acquitted, the Supreme Court of Victoria finding that there was no assault. The woman's consent was real. There was no fraud as to the nature and quality of the doctor's act (*R v Mobilio* (1991)).

This decision, which seems bizarre to many, was the legacy of an old English case, *R v Clarence* (1988). Clarence was infected with gonorrhoea. He knew it, although his wife did not. He had sexual intercourse with her. She contracted the infection. He was prosecuted.

It was said that he had assaulted his wife. Nonsense, he said: consent is a defence to assault. She's a grown woman, and she knew exactly what she was consenting to—namely sexual intercourse. The prosecution responded that her consent was not real, and that had she known that he was infected she would not have agreed to sex. The appeal court was no doubt worried about the dire social consequences of suggesting that a wife (who shared, per the Bible, one body with her husband) might have any excuse not to have sex at the husband's whim. It agreed with Clarence. Mrs Clarence had consented to an act of the 'nature and quality' of that which had occurred.

Clarence continued to wreak injustice in England until 2004, when, in the context of transmission of HIV, it was finally held that where one does not know but a sexual partner has a sexually transmissible infection, consent to sex (*R v Dica* (2004)). Another way of putting it is that the court looks more to the mind of the defendant than to the state of knowledge of the victim in deciding on liability in sexual assault cases. That's no surprise.

That's the criminal law. Medical gropers are less safe from prison than they were. If you're going to touch someone, whether in the course of a medical consultation or otherwise, you will do so criminally unless you do it with their express or implied consent, and that consent will not be real (at least in a sexual context) unless the real reason for the touching is what the patient thinks it is.

But the criminal law, slanted towards acquittal as it must be, is necessarily more forgiving to defendants than the civil law. If you're convicted of a criminal offence your liberty is in jeopardy. If you're found liable for a civil wrong, at most your wallet, and perhaps your reputation, will be. A lower quality of consent is required to exculpate in the criminal law than in the civil law.

The whole notion of 'informed consent' permeates, and sometimes paralyses, medical practice. 'Informed consent' itself is a US idea, but, like so many ideas, it has crossed the Atlantic and metastasized throughout Europe and the common-law world. It's got a good pedigree. We can argue about the age of that pedigree, but a sensible point to start is 1957, when the California Court of Appeals stated that 'a physician violates his duty to the plaintiff and subjects himself to liability if he withholds any facts which are necessary to form the basis of an intelligent consent by the patient to the proposed treatment' (*Salgo v Leland Stanford Jr University Board of Trustees* (1957)).

The US courts built on this and other observations a massive edifice that supposedly protects patients, and certainly terrifies doctors. In the enormously influential case of *Canterbury v Spence* (1972), a US District Court observed that the doctor's duty was not merely a duty to answer questions, but a duty to volunteer information. Rejecting conclusively the operation of the English *Bolam* test in the law of consent, the court held that the right to self-determination was so crucial that the law, rather than doctors themselves, should set the required standard. The doctor must disclose all 'material risks'. A risk is material when 'a reasonable person, in what the physician knows or should know to be the patient's position, would be likely to attach significance to the risk or cluster of risks in deciding whether or not to forgo the proposed therapy'. Only where disclosure of the risks would pose 'a serious threat of psychological detriment to the patient' could non-disclosure be justified.

The Canadians agree (*Reibl v Hughes* (1980)). So do the Australians (*Rogers v Whittaker* (1992)).

The English law in the area is harder to describe. The leading case is *Sidaway v Board of Governors of the Bethlem Royal Hospital and the Maudsley Hospital* (1985), but it's terribly difficult to work out what it says.

There were five judges, and four very different judgments. There has been a tendency to read only those judgments supporting the notion that the *Bolam* test applies (and accordingly that the doctor will have discharged his obligation if he counsels the patient in a way that would be endorsed by a responsible body of medical opinion). But English lawyers are beginning to read and apply the other judgments—and in particular those which hint at the US way of looking at things: see *Pearce v United Bristol Healthcare NHS Trust* (1999). In any event, professional regulatory codes are increasingly using the US language of informed consent, and if that's the case, it's hard to say that *Bolam*-responsible UK doctors shouldn't feel obliged to treat their patients as if they practised in New York.

There's another reason, too, why Europe is becoming more and more wedded to the notion of 'informed consent' as understood in the US. That's the European Convention on Human Rights. Article 8 of the Convention robustly protects patient autonomy. Even if *Bolam* doesn't insist on full disclosure, Article 8 may do so—unless it can be contended under Article 8(2) that such insistence is likely to gum up the health-care system to the overall detriment of society.

In fact such a contention isn't fanciful. Full disclosure of risks sounds fine, but is it possible? And if it is possible, is it practicable?

Every drug ever produced, and every procedure ever devised, has actual or potential complications, some of them vanishingly rare and recorded only in highly obscure journals. It's simply not possible to run through them all. And if it were, it's neither practicable (it would leave no time for any treatment at all) nor desirable (because many people would be scared stiff by the mention of a horrifying but almost unknown possibility, and would irrationally decline treatment, or be inappropriately worried while undergoing it). Some sort of balance needs to be struck between full disclosure and sensible disclosure. It may be that the balancing exercise demanded by Article 8 is the sensible way to strike that balance.

But perhaps there is another, even more fundamental, reason to be less dumbstruck than we often are by our awe of informed consent. And that is that it's not possible to identify the *person* who's really giving consent. By all means respect autonomy: a system that doesn't do so is malignant. But ask: 'Whose autonomy?' Consider a person who is faced with a decision about whether to have life-prolonging treatment for cancer. The biological man may want to cling onto life with the help of any available technology. The sentimental family man might want to see his children for those extra few months. The considerate family man might want to die early so as 'not to be a burden' to his family. The man who has read John Stuart Mill and drafted a 'life-plan' might want to die as he has lived, with a proud independence unfettered by morphine and incontinence. The religious man might think that sophisticated therapy frustrates the will of God. And so on. Few of us are, at least when it comes to ontological challenge, well-integrated people. We'll be one person one minute, and another the next.

The consequences of failing to obtain the patient's consent

One example makes the point. You go to your dentist. He tells you that a lot of work needs to be done, and that if it's not, the consequences for your dental health will be dire. You sign a form agreeing to the treatment. He drills and fills. You pay him.

Criminal consequences

If the treatment was unnecessary, and the dentist knew it, he has procured your consent by fraud. He might try to run a *Clarence*-type argument (saying that you knew the nature and quality of what you consented to), but he's likely to fail. Quite apart from committing an offence of dishonesty, which could have its own criminal consequences, he has assaulted you, and can be prosecuted in the criminal courts. If there was a sexual motive, of course (if he'd gassed and groped you), he can be prosecuted too.

Civil consequences

Assault is a civil wrong too. Touching someone without their (sufficient) consent is an assault/battery. If the treatment was, to the dentist's knowledge, unnecessary, he can be sued for damages for assault.

But perhaps your dentist was not dishonest. Perhaps he should just have given you a better explanation than he did of the risks and benefits of the treatment. In the US and many other places you're entitled to know the material risks. It's negligent not to explain them. Your autonomy rights have been outraged. The way the law looks at such negligence in consent cases is complex: it's discussed in Chapter 6. It's enough to say here that it may be possible to get damages representing the consequences of that negligence.

Disciplinary consequences

The dentist is accountable to his regulatory body. He is obliged to comply with a set of professional standards. Depending on the facts, he may have breached those obligations. This may have put his registration at risk, or attracted some other disciplinary sanction.

Chapter 6
Clinical negligence

Doctors, being human, make mistakes. Since doctors' business is with human bodies, and human bodies are really rather important for much of the business of living, loving, and earning, those mistakes can be far-reaching and expensive.

But does that mean that an honest mistake by a well-meaning doctor should give an injured patient a right to sue? If so, what yardstick should be used in deciding that a doctor has fallen short of the mark? If a doctor has made a mistake, should all consequent damage, however remote, and however amorphous, be placed at the doctor's door?

This is the world of clinical negligence—a term that makes the eyes of many (and in particular Americans) roll. To many it speaks of shiny-suited, ambulance-chasing, claim-inflating lawyers, whose greed makes clinicians and insurers tremble, and causes patients to be hysterically over-investigated in an effort to see off the litigators. Clinical negligence claims are agonizing for everyone but the lawyers. The lawyers should be impoverished if they can be. But it's hard to get rid of them completely.

'No fault' or tort?

In theory the clinical negligence industry isn't inevitable. The state, or a consortium of insurers, could simply decide that they will pay out compensation on a no-fault basis to the victims of medical mistakes without the need for the elaborate and expensive ballet of the courts. But in practice this rarely happens. There are two main reasons. The first is the sheer expense that would be involved in such a scheme. In the UK, today, a baby whose cerebral palsy has been caused by obstetric negligence could get an award of £10 million—reflecting a lifetime's loss of earnings, the need for a lifetime's care, therapy, equipment, and so on.

Suppose there's a modest (25 per cent) chance of avoiding a £10 million liability. To get that chance you've got to go into the casino (it's called a court). Most casinos have an entrance fee, and this one certainly does. It's made up of lawyers' fees, expert witness costs, and many other elements. But even with the sleekest lawyers, the most eminent experts, and the 75 per cent probability of having to pay all of the claimant's costs too, it will often be financially sensible to pay the entrance fee, spin the wheel, and see if that one in four chance comes up.

The second reason why no-fault schemes are unattractive in the clinical negligence context is the frequent difficulty of establishing causation. A no-fault scheme in relation to road traffic accidents is one thing. If car A hits car B, and the occupants of car B get hurt, it's often not hard to attribute that hurt to car A. But in clinical negligence claims causation is often much murkier. Many cases end with the defendant having been found to be in breach of duty, but with the claimant failing to prove that that breach of duty has caused any loss. No-fault schemes have to presume that causation is straightforward. You can't do that in medicine. Cells and enzymes are less predictable than trucks.

The New Zealand experience illustrates this well. New Zealand has a no-fault scheme of compensation for medical injuries, but it requires a claimant to prove that her injury was caused by 'medical or surgical misadventure'. Many clinical negligence claims in tort jurisdictions are concerned solely and agonizingly with precisely that.

Other supposedly no-fault schemes in fact find themselves edging back towards fault. Sweden is a good example. Fault, it insists, is irrelevant: claimants are compensated for injuries that result from inaction on the part of a clinician that is 'medically unjustified'. But to argue about whether something is medically unjustified is, very often, to argue about whether the doctor is at fault.

Tort is surprisingly hard to escape.

The elements of a clinical negligence claim in tort

Just as in any negligence claim in a tort-based system, to be successful in a clinical negligence claim in tort a claimant must prove that:

- the defendant owed him a duty of care
- there has been a breach of that duty
- the breach has caused damage
- of a type recognized by the law of tort.

Claims in contract

Private medicine is performed according to contracts. The relevant contract will often be between the patient and the doctor who provides the care. The position is sometimes complicated by the involvement of medical insurers and private hospitals: it may therefore be that a contract exists between the insurer and a hospital, rather than the patient and the doctor.

In the simple situation of a contract for treatment between the patient and a doctor, the contract, in practice, adds little or nothing to the law of tort. Many countries (for instance France, Belgium, Germany, Austria, Switzerland, and Greece) use contractual models for establishing the liability of a doctor, but the courts in all jurisdictions have been very reluctant to read the governing contract as anything other than an agreement by the doctor to use the skill and care reasonably to be expected of a doctor holding himself out as having the expertise of the defendant. The law of tort makes an identical demand. In particular the courts are unhappy about construing an agreement as an agreement for a particular medical or surgical result—for instance a cure of the patient's cancer, or a pair of breasts that look like the ones in the surgeon's brochure. This is because they recognize the vagaries of biology. The clinician never has complete control, and so it is unfair for a contract to assume that he does.

This is not to say that analogies with contract aren't sometimes enlightening. Sometimes they are—and particularly in relation to the question of damages for loss of a chance. As we shall see.

Duty of care

The existence of a duty of care is seldom an issue in medical cases. By and large there is no obligation to be a Good Samaritan. When the tannoy pleads 'Is there a doctor in the house?' the doctor can sit quietly and ignore it. In most (but not all) jurisdictions he will be safe from the law, if not from his conscience, if he watches an entirely salvageable patient die. Doctors, in short, usually owe duties only to their patients, and can decide who is their patient and who isn't.

Usually it's obvious when someone is a patient of a particular clinician, and of course clinicians have a duty to take reasonable care of 'their' patients. Often several clinicians will owe a duty to a single patient. In a state health-care system the appropriate defendant will usually be the statutory provider (for instance the National Health Service Trust or the hospital) which employs the clinicians directly responsible for the patient's care.

Very occasionally, though, there are arguments about the existence of a duty.

Imagine, for instance, that a doctor is employed by an insurance company. His job is to look through the medical notes of potential clients to see if they are a good insurance risk. He is looking through X's notes when he discovers a clear indication that X is suffering from an entirely curable cancer. It is plain that X's own clinicians have missed the cancer. What should the doctor do? Does he have to tell X what he has found, so that X can get the necessary treatment?

Or suppose that a surgeon performs a vasectomy on Boy, and then, negligently, assures him that he is sterile and need take no more contraceptive precautions. Boy later meets Girl. Over wine and dinner in a candlelit restaurant, Boy romantically assures Girl that he is sterile. Accordingly Girl has unprotected sex with Boy. The assurance was wrong, and Girl becomes pregnant. Can Girl sue the surgeon?

There is wide variation between jurisdictions as to how these issues are resolved. But most countries use a formula akin to the English one, asking whether the relationship between the claimant and the defendant is sufficiently close, whether the damage suffered by the claimant is a foreseeable result of the defendant's negligence (a test more obviously at home in the law of causation, but which has had a home in the law relating to duties at least since the canonical case of *Donoghue v Stevenson* (1932)—the one about the snail in the ginger beer bottle), and whether it is just and reasonable to impose such a duty on the defendant: see *Caparo Industries plc v Dickman* (1990). Policy considerations play a big part in the determination—particularly in relation to this third element.

The insurance company case would be difficult to call, but many judges would find that the doctor's duty was restricted to the duty he owed by contract to the employing insurer (compare *Kapfunde v Abbey National plc* (1999)). The vasectomy case is a real example: the English Court of Appeal held that one could not owe a duty to all the potential sexual partners of a patient, and accordingly that Girl had no claim: *Goodwill v British Pregnancy Advisory Services* (1996).

This doesn't mean that a doctor cannot owe a duty to unknown third parties.

A psychotic patient tells his psychiatrist that, if released from his secure hospital, he will kill the first person he sees. The psychiatrist negligently discharges the patient and, true to his promise, the patient strangles, on the hospital steps, the first passer-by he sees.

Could the victim's family sue the psychiatrist? Almost certainly: see *Tarasoff v The Regents of the University of California* (1976); *Palmer v South Tees Health Authority* (1999). What if the victim were the second person the patient saw? Very likely. Or the twentieth? Very probably.

Can it not be said that there's a duty to *any* victim? That goes directly against authorities like the vasectomy case (*Goodwill*). But to say otherwise is to give a negligent doctor an immunity simply because the patient has been incautious enough to blurt out his plans. Why should that blurt have the effect of restricting the doctor's duty? Shouldn't it rather have made the release *more* negligent? The doctor has loosed into society a deadly weapon which might go off at any moment with obviously foreseeable loss of life. Shouldn't the law have something to say about that?

The answer is that the law should and does, but what it says is stuttering and inconsistent. This is a fast-evolving area. The next big steps in that evolution are likely to occur in relation to the liability for damage done by psychiatric patients, liability for transmission of HIV or other sexually transmitted diseases by sexual partners of a doctor's patient, and liability for psychiatric injury to people other than patients.

This sort of psychiatric injury is common. A father might watch the delivery of his dead child—dead through the negligence of the obstetrician—and be traumatized as a result. A mother might be depressed by the burdens of bringing up a negligently brain-damaged child. The worry about compensating these apparently deserving claimants is that it will open the floodgates to a tsunami of claims. Many people far removed from the scene of the tort can be mentally affected in various ways by clinical negligence.

Various devices are used to keep the floodgates shut, including a requirement that a claimant is in a close relationship to the patient, or has witnessed the 'immediate aftermath' of the negligence.

Breach of duty

In England and many other jurisdictions the test for breach of duty is the *Bolam* test (see *Bolam v Friern Hospital Management Committee* (1957)). This says that a professional will be in breach of duty if what they have done would not be endorsed by any responsible body of opinion in the relevant specialty. It is a test both of substantive law and of evidence, and has become ubiquitous in professional negligence law, being used to determine the liability of everyone from heart surgeons to plumbers (who, after all, have a lot in common).

It has sometimes been abused by defendants and defendant-friendly judges, some of whom, seeing any attack on fellow professionals as a general attack on the middle classes, have been happy to acquit a doctor of negligence on the basis of the evidence of another doctor who, having miraculously remained on the register for an undistinguished professional lifetime, is prepared to say (at £200 an hour) not that *he* would have done an operation in the way that the defendant did, but that he once met someone in the golf club who'd also astonishingly escaped erasure who did it that way.

Claimants rightly railed against this. Their complaints led, in England, to a revisiting of the test in *Bolitho v City and Hackney Health Authority* (1998), in which the court pointed out something that had tended to be forgotten—namely that the old test referred to *responsible* opinion. There may be cases, it said, where, notwithstanding evidence that the defendant adopted a common practice, the defendant might still be negligent—if the practice did not stand up to logical scrutiny.

This provoked howls of worry from doctors, concerned that their professional practices would be second-guessed by medically unqualified judges. To many, those howls sounded petulant. The doctors were really insisting that they and only they should set the standards by which they should be judged. And if you are the law, aren't you above the law?

It was precisely those concerns that had made other jurisdictions reject the *Bolam* approach and leave the setting of legal standards in the hands of the courts. The best examples relate to the law of consent: see below.

Bolam is on the retreat. *Bolitho* chased it into its proper place, but medicine itself has eroded *Bolam*'s authority significantly. Medicine is increasingly evidence-based. Proper medical practice is increasingly based on large, statistically significant studies of efficacy which are embodied in clinical guidelines. There's a diminishing amount of room for opinion. If the literature conclusively shows that practice X is better than practice Y, then (economic considerations aside) how can anyone *responsibly* adopt practice Y?

Consent cases occupy a curious corner of the clinical negligence world. They are very common. A patient might, for instance, say that she was not appropriately warned about the risks of surgery, that had she been warned she would not have consented to it, and accordingly that she would have been spared the damage wrought by the surgery.

Even in jurisdictions where *Bolam* rules, it is not self-evident, according to a number of eminent authorities, that the test for liability in relation to allegedly negligent consenting of a patient should be the *Bolam* test. In the leading English authority, *Sidaway v Board of Governors of the Bethlem Royal Hospital* (1984), a case whose effect is famously obscure, the House of Lords, while upholding the broad proposition that the *Bolam* test applied, did so cautiously, suggesting that judges might be more ready than in other classes of case to make up their own minds about whether the doctor in question had done what was necessary.

Lord Scarman, dissenting, approved the position in the US case of *Canterbury v Spence* (1972), in which the US court, while not saying that evidence about medical practice was irrelevant to the question of what amounted to appropriate care, insisted that the court, and not the medical profession, was the arbiter. Lord Scarman was embraced in several Commonwealth countries. Even in conservative England he's slowly being rehabilitated. Ever since *Canterbury v Spence*, *Bolam*, cold-shouldered elsewhere, has been shown emphatically to the door in consent cases in Canada (see *Reibl v Hughes* (1980)), Australia (*F v R* (1983)), and South Africa (*Castell v De Greef* (1994)).

Canterbury v Spence articulated the 'reasonable patient' test, which we met in Chapter 5. Material risks must be disclosed. A risk is material if it would be regarded as significant by a reasonable person in the patient's position. There's an exception, inconsistently recognized by judges across the world, and apparently frowned on by some professional regulatory bodies:

this is the 'therapeutic privilege'—the notion that information can be withheld if to disclose it might be psychologically harmful.

Once a revolution starts, it's difficult to stop. If the unthinkable could be thought in relation to consent cases, why stop there? Why not abolish all reference and all deference to expert medical evidence in all clinical negligence cases, and let the law do the job (which many presume is its only, or at least main, job) of setting standards?

That was indeed the view of Gaudron J in the High Court of Australia case, *Rogers v Whittaker* (1992):

> ...even in the area of diagnosis and treatment, there is, in my view, no legal basis for limiting liability in terms of the rule known as 'the *Bolam* test'...[I]t may be a convenient statement of the approach dictated by the state of the evidence in some cases. As such, it may have some utility as a rule of thumb in some jury cases, but it can serve no other useful function...

This was fighting talk. It was not adopted by the majority of the court in *Rogers v Whittaker*, who restricted their restriction of *Bolam* to counselling cases, observing that 'There is a fundamental difference between, on the one hand, diagnosis and treatment and, on the other hand, the provision of advice and information to the patient...Because the choice to be made calls for a decision by the patient on information known to the medical practitioner but not to the patient, it would be illogical to hold that the amount of information to be provided by the medical practitioner can be determined from the perspective of the practitioner alone or, for that matter, of the medical profession.'

There are many who would like to see *Bolam* excised wholly from the law books—and not just those sections that relate to counselling. For them, *Bolam* stinks of medical paternalism; of the closing of the white-coated professional ranks against the desperate patient.

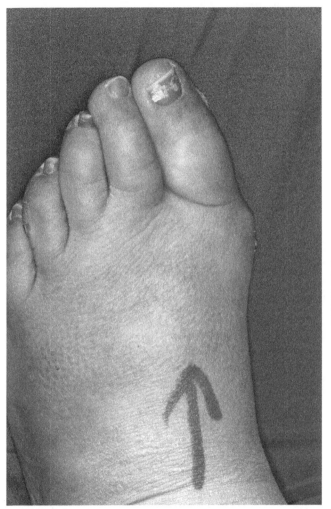

5. A surgical site marked up to avoid confusion. However forgiving *Bolam* might be, there is no responsible body of medical opinion which operates on the wrong finger, arm, or leg

But despite the political, sociological, and jurisprudential objections to *Bolam*, and despite *Bolam* being ousted from its throne by the evidence-based medicine revolution, it is hard to imagine that it will vanish altogether. It can't. The judges need it—especially in cases of diagnosis and treatment.

Consent cases are rather different. They are really about patients' human rights, and judges, being, by and large, human, are qualified to opine about whether or not human rights have been breached. But questions of diagnosis and treatment are technically complicated. Something akin to the *Bolam* approach will inevitably persist, simply because judges aren't equipped to make judgements about the appropriateness of a particular medical approach without the help of expert evidence. The nature of that inevitable help will inevitably boil down to something like *Bolam*. Just as judges aren't equipped to decide, without the benefit of expert evidence, which medical approach is correct, so they're not equipped, in most cases, to decide which of two competing medical approaches (the claimant's and the defendant's) is the right one in the relevant clinical circumstances. Should they decide on the basis of the cut of the expert's suit, or the number of peer-reviewed publications that each has to his name? Of course not. And hence there will have to be an appeal to a standard along the lines of 'a responsible body of medical opinion'. *Bolam* has lost some status, but it's far from dead.

Causation

The basic rule: 'but-for' causation

However rankly negligent a defendant has been, the claim will fail unless some loss has been caused. The basic test sounds common-sensical: it is for the claimant to show that, but for the defendant's negligence, she would have been spared the injury that she has in fact suffered.

So: a patient attends her family doctor, worried about a lump in her breast. The doctor examines the lump and wrongly reassures her that it is benign. In fact she should have been referred for further investigation. Had she been, breast cancer would have been diagnosed, and treatment would have been started. Her chances of complete cure at that point would have been 49 per cent. By the time her breast cancer is diagnosed, the chance of cure has dropped to 5 per cent.

The doctor admits breach of duty, but the claim, insofar as it is a claim for loss of cure, fails. Statistically the patient was doomed at the time of the first consultation. The doctor's negligence is causally irrelevant.

Loss of a chance

This conclusion troubles many. Hasn't the doctor deprived the patient of something that is capable of grounding a claim in tort? The law commonly compensates claimants who, because of breach of contract, lose a chance of gaining a benefit or avoiding a detriment. In an old English case, a girl paid money to a newspaper in order to enter a beauty contest. Due to the paper's administrative incompetence (in breach of its contract with her), she was not entered into the contest, and was therefore deprived of her chance (which would not have been better than evens) of winning it. She was entitled to damages: *Chaplin v Hicks* (1911). If a solicitor's incompetence robs a client of a (say) 30 per cent chance of succeeding in litigation, it is no answer for the solicitor to say: 'You'd probably have lost anyway, so there's no claim against me.' And yet that is precisely the assertion that lets the negligent doctor escape.

Why the discrepancy? Some would say that there is no discrepancy, pointing to the fact that the newspaper and the solicitor are acting under a contract, and that one might construe those contracts as contracts to take reasonable care to give the client the very chance of which she has been deprived. But many medical services are provided under contract. Can those contracts not be read in an identical way? And if so, is it acceptable to deprive a National Health Service patient of a remedy when a private patient, in identical circumstances, would get compensation? Some would contend that there's a difference between the chance of obtaining a benefit (as in the newspaper and litigation case) and the chance of avoiding a detriment (as in the breast cancer case). But that doesn't work either, for many reasons, one of which is that it is legal child's play to transform a benefit into a detriment, and vice versa. Who would like to tell the cancer victim that she hadn't really been deprived of the benefit of living and seeing her children grow up, but had instead merely failed to avoid the detriment of death? Nothing of any moral substance (and surely the breast cancer case has moral substance in spadefuls) should turn on such distinctions. It brings the law into disrepute.

What is operating here is not logic, but policy, and it would be better for the law's reputation if that were frankly admitted. The policy, in fact, is a sound, pragmatic one. We've seen it already in other contexts: the courts would be hopelessly clogged if damages for a lost chance were routinely allowed in clinical negligence cases. Many (arguably most) medical mistakes cause a patient to lose a chance of *something*. If loss of a chance were sufficient to allow a claimant to recover damages, one might effectively be doing away with the requirement to prove causation at all in clinical negligence cases: a breach of duty would be followed by judgment for damages to be assessed. Perhaps that sounds just. But the vagaries of biology being what they are, quantifying loss is often nightmarishly difficult and expensive. Whether the difficulties of some cases should defeat justice in all is a literally moot point.

Material contribution to injury and risk of injury

The law doesn't always run scared from biological uncertainty. Sometimes it recognizes that defendants shouldn't always be able to shelter behind the statement 'This situation is terribly complex'—effectively getting a windfall from the sometimes banal simplicity of the 'but-for' test.

Take an industrial disease case. Over a working lifetime, during the course of his work for several employers, the claimant has inhaled noxious dust. Some employers were negligent in letting him inhale it; some were not. He gets a disabling lung disease, and seeks compensation. He sues the negligent employers. They respond: 'The but-for test applies. You cannot prove that but for our "guilty" dust you would not have the disease. Who knows exactly what the trigger was, or when the threshold was reached? The innocent dust might have triggered the disease.'

The law, generally, doesn't like this response. Most jurisdictions have developed a way of compensating a claimant in this position—often by saying that it is sufficient for a claimant to prove that the defendant's negligence has materially contributed to his injury (*Bailey v Ministry of Defence* (2009)). Sometimes it goes further, holding that, in some circumstances, a material increase in the risk of a condition will be enough (if the claimant has in fact developed that condition): *McGhee v National Coal Board* (1973).

Many situations in medical law are analogous to these industrial disease cases. A vulnerable brain might have been exposed to negligent and non-negligent periods of hypoxia, for instance. Or the state of medical knowledge might be such that the experts cannot say that a negligent act probably caused the injury, but are happy to say that it increased the risk of it. While the policy considerations that dictate caution in loss-of-chance cases make the courts wary of accepting analogies with industrial disease, the law in many places is evolving towards acceptance.

Consent cases

From the point of view of causation, consent cases might look easy. Suppose that a surgeon negligently fails to warn about the risks of a proposed operation. Had the patient been appropriately warned, she would not have consented to the operation. The operation goes ahead, and in the course of it, or afterwards, as a result of it, the patient suffers injury.

The but-for test has no problem with such a case. Whether or not the injuries were those about which the surgeon should have warned the patient, they wouldn't have occurred but for the negligence, and (subject to the rules about remoteness—see below) causation is usually established.

But wait a moment. Take the following case. Its facts are not unusual.

A patient goes to see a consultant spinal surgeon. She needs a laminectomy to decompress her spinal cord. The surgeon fails to warn her about a 1 per cent risk of urinary incontinence. She agrees to the operation. The operation is done entirely competently, but the 1 per cent risk eventuates, and the patient is left incontinent. She sues the surgeon. The court finds that had she been properly warned, she would have consented to the operation, but would have pondered for a bit before consenting, and accordingly would not have had the procedure on the day that she had it. Since the 1 per cent risk hovers over every patient undergoing the procedure (and just happened to alight on her when she in fact had the operation), a short delay would probably have meant that she avoided it. So: same surgeon, same counselling, same operation, same operating table, different day. Does she succeed? And if so, should she?

The but-for test, narrowly applied, says that she does and should. And indeed she did in a controversial English case: *Chester v Afshar* (2005) (although not simply on a 'but-for' basis). But many are outraged by this result. The connection between the surgeon's negligence and the damage suffered by the patient is mistily metaphysical.

There's a better way to see such cases. The patient did indeed suffer harm, but it was harm not to the nerves supplying her bladder, but to her right to be properly informed—her autonomy right. Violations of human rights, even when they don't involve physical harm, are routinely compensated.

Hypothetical causation

Very often clinical negligence claims involve omissions rather than acts. A clinician negligently fails to attend a patient, or fails to arrange a particular investigation. The court then has to determine what would have happened had the clinician attended or the investigation been performed. Usually these questions turn on the but-for test, or a gloss on that test along the lines of material contribution. But commonly things are more complicated.

An example. A paediatrician negligently fails to answer her bleep. As a result a baby suffers an episode of hypoxic brain damage which leaves it irreversibly disabled. The expert evidence is that the only intervention that would have prevented the damage would have been the immediate insertion of a tube into the baby's trachea. But the paediatrician says (and the court accepts) that, had she attended, she would not have intubated the baby. The court finds that a responsible body of paediatricians would not have intubated—in other words that it would not have been negligent for the paediatrician, had she come, to have failed to give the only treatment that would have prevented the injury.

Does the claimant succeed? In England, and many other places which hallow *Bolam*, she does not: see *Bolitho v City and Hackney Health Authority* (1998). The question is whether, but for the negligence, injury would have been avoided, and negligence is defined according to the *Bolam* test. The negligence here is causally irrelevant: nothing different would have happened had the doctor rushed diligently to the ward.

This is not the only way of looking at it. The pressure on the non-attending doctor to convince herself (and therefore the court) that she would not have given the only effective treatment must be intense. One might argue that the law should compensate for that pressure by assuming that the doctor would give effective treatment. That argument is easier in a jurisdiction that is not in thrall to *Bolam*. If *Bolam* rules absolutely in the law of breach of duty, it is hard to stop it holding sway over causation too.

Damage of a sort recognized by the law

There is a lot of negligence by doctors, but there are few clinical negligence cases. One of many important reasons for this is that most of the negligence doesn't cause loss of a type that the law thinks should be compensated: it is usually hurt feelings, upset, or inconvenience.

A patient goes into hospital for a corneal graft. After the operation the surgeon comes to see him on the ward. The good news, says the surgeon, is that the operation went very well, and the patient's sight will be restored. The bad news, however, is that the hospital's tissue bank has just told him that the cornea came from a patient who, many years before, had had syphilis. It's unfortunate that this wasn't picked up by the tissue bank: it should have been. But, the surgeon goes on, there's no need to worry. There is no case reported in the literature of anyone contracting syphilis this way, but just to be absolutely safe, the patient will be given a course of prophylactic antibiotics.

The patient walks out of hospital (for the first time in years not bumping into things as he does so), and sues the hospital.

But what's the loss? The patient doesn't have syphilis, and will never get it. He's just been rather shaken up by the whole experience of being told about the origin of the cornea. No psychiatrist will give that 'shaking up' the label of a recognized psychiatric illness.

In most jurisdictions this claim would fail. There's negligence, the negligence has caused *something*, but the something is not in one of the categories of compensable damage.

This isn't because upset, worry, and so on are too nebulous to be quantified. Pain, loss of amenity, and loss of reputation are no easier to value, but are routinely valued in the courts. Rather it is, again, policy. A minimum threshold of severity is arbitrarily imposed to stop the courts from being swamped by claims.

Assessing quantum

Compensation in negligence cases aims to put the claimant in the position in which she would have been had the defendant not been negligent. In a typical clinical negligence claim there are several elements.

'Pain, suffering, and loss of amenity' are valued by reference to published guidelines and reported cases. In England, for instance, quadriplegia was typically valued in 2013 between £255,000 and £317,500, and the loss of a leg below the knee at £177,000–£104,500.

Then there are the heads of claim that are, in theory, capable of more scientific quantification: loss of earnings, travel expenses, the cost of aids and appliances, and the cost of care. Life expectancy (assessed either in relation to the individual patient or, if the patient is likely to die at the time predicted by the actuaries, by reference to population mortality data) is used to calculate the number of years over which future loss will run—a number discounted to take account of presumptions about the amount of money that the sum of damages, invested, will yield. It's a laborious process.

Perhaps clinical negligence lawyers deserve their fees after all.

Chapter 7
Research on human subjects

The world looked at what Mengele and the other Nazi doctors had done, and said 'Never again.' In fact the Nazis were (as some of them pointed out in their subsequent trials) in a long, dishonourable, and well-established tradition of abusive medical research. J. Marion Sims, in the 1840s, repeatedly operated on unanesthetized slave women; Leo Stanley, in the first half of the 20th century, implanted pig, goat, and sheep testicles into prisoners; and countless patients in many countries were deliberately infected with deadly and disabling diseases in the name of science.

From Auschwitz, to Helsinki, to the African bush

The immediate response to the revelations from Auschwitz, Buchenwald, and elsewhere was the Nuremberg Code (1947), which declared that the consent of all participants to all research on them was essential, and the Declaration of Geneva (1948), which set out doctors' ethical duties towards their patients.

The Nuremberg Code gave way to the World Medical Association's Declaration of Helsinki (1964). This has gone through six revisions. The latest was in 2008. It has no legal force in itself, but has had profound influence on national and international research ethics and law. As we've seen, authoritative ethical guidance has a way of becoming actual or de facto medical law. Most countries have given at least a nod to the Declaration—or at least to some version of it—and so the best way of identifying the international legal consensus is to look at it.

It has done a lot to change the thoughtlessly utilitarian or downright callous ethos of pre-war medical research. But not enough. Mengele-esque abuses continued. In Tuskegee, Alabama (1932–72), syphilis patients were told that they were being treated for syphilis. They weren't, although they could have been. Many died; many fathered children with congenital syphilis. In Staten Island, until 1966, mentally disabled children were secretly infected with viral hepatitis. Until 1971, women attending a contraception clinic in San Antonio were given placebos instead of effective drugs, without their consent. There were several pregnancies. Between 1960 and 1971 the US Department of Defense and the Defense Atomic Support Agency funded whole-body irradiation experiments on non-consenting patients. A 1994 study showed that a drug called zidovudine was extremely effective in reducing mother–infant HIV transmission. Some subsequent trials withheld the drug from patients in Third World countries, while ensuring that US patients had it. And so it went on.

The Declaration, in its present form, emphasizes the importance of autonomy and informed consent, and insists that the subject's welfare outweighs the welfare of society or the march of science.

The Declaration is a well-meaning document. It's an honest attempt to protect the rights of individuals while at the same time acknowledging that scientific progress is crucial, and that a communitarian perspective sometimes makes sense. But it's hard to be philosophically consistent if you're that ambitious, and the Declaration isn't consistent. It's a patchwork quilt, not seamlessly woven from the yarn of one principle. That in itself isn't a criticism. Some of the best law is made from several philosophical materials. But since the Declaration does pay explicit lip service to autonomy, it's worth observing that it outlaws research on humans unless the importance of the objective outweighs the inherent risks and burdens to the subject (Article 21). That's a highly paternalistic restriction. If a pharmaceutical company wants to pay me a huge amount of money to participate in potentially dangerous research that might lead to the development of a new brand of shampoo, why shouldn't it be able to do so? Isn't my body my own (unless I choose to engage in rado-maroditic bondage: see Chapter 5)?

The Declaration has evolved very significantly through its many revisions. Many of the revisions have generated hot and anxious debate. Here's why.

Imagine that you're the head of a multinational pharmaceutical company. You have the patent for a very promising drug for the treatment of malaria. Malaria is very important. It kills millions each year, almost all of them in the poorer countries of the world. If the drug works, your share price and your bonus will rocket.

The efficacy of the drug needs to be established. That means clinical trials in hot, poor places.

The most scientifically satisfactory results (which would lead to the fastest acceptance of the drug by the market) would be obtained by trials in which a large cohort of infected patients in a remote part of Africa, all of whom need treatment, is divided into two. Half would receive the drug; half would receive a pharmacologically inert placebo. It would be a 'double blind' trial, in which neither the patients nor the administrators of the drug/placebo knew who was getting the drug and who the placebo.

But there's a problem. Patients receiving the placebo are likely to die. That's a shame. It's also avoidable. There are already drugs available which would stop them dying.

What should be done?

The answer's not obvious. If this trial is vetoed on the grounds that it's unethical, no one at all will get treatment. Many of them will die. Certainly (if the drug is as good as it is thought to be), more will die than would die if the trial happened. Wouldn't the potential participants prefer a 50 per cent chance of salvation to a 0 per cent chance? And, since the alternative trial methods, not involving the ethically dubious placebo group, won't produce such a clear result, there will be a longer delay before the drug is commercially available—so leading to the loss of more lives.

If those essentially utilitarian arguments hold water, is there anything to be said against entirely non-consensual research on the same cohorts? Every participant might think that they're receiving, say, a free drink of lemonade, but in fact they're getting either the drug or the placebo. The science would be good, lives would be saved. What's the problem?

I don't seek to adjudicate. The Declaration is unhappy about either version of the malaria trial. It disapproves of placebo-controlled trials except where there is no intervention that is known to work, or where, for 'compelling and scientifically good methodological reasons', a placebo control is necessary and patients who receive a placebo or no treatment will not be subject to any risk of serious or irreversible harm (Article 32). The Declaration cautions that '[e]xtreme care must be taken to avoid abuse of this option'. The US Food and Drug Administration has refused to be bound by these limitations—essentially on the grounds that they hamstring science, which isn't in the world's ultimate interest.

Subsequent revisions sought to meet these concerns by providing that research is only justified if there is a reasonable likelihood that the 'population or community' in which the research is carried out stands to benefit from the results of the research (Article 17), and that when a study is completed participants should be provided with whatever the study has shown to be the best thing for their situation (Article 33).

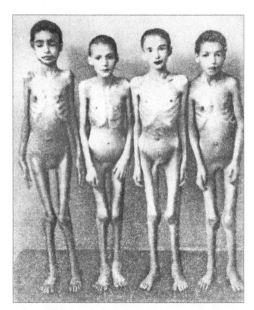

6. **Twins at Auschwitz, used for medical experiments by the Nazi doctor Josef Mengele. The horrors of the Nazi regime have had a profound influence on modern attitudes towards experiments on humans**

When the only hope is in the Unknown

The Declaration is rightly conservative. It talks a lot about the proper communication of risks to research subjects. Usually, when a trial of a novel product begins, there will be *some* evidence to suggest that it will work. But that's not always so: there's still some genuine pharmacological mystery in the world.

A drug company has been working for years on a new drug for colon cancer. The drug has done exciting things in mice. It shrinks their metastases to nothing, bringing them back from the grave. But then we're not mice, or not necessarily so. The next step is to test it in humans. But the pharmacologists are worried: it might cure, but it might kill or maim. Can it be tested? Or must the clinical trial go on hold unless and until the researchers can show that the risk of death or serious injury is as low as you'd expect it to be in a trial of healthy volunteers?

The Declaration is pragmatic. We'd want it to be. If the options are certain death from cancer or a 50 per cent chance of cure associated with a 50 per cent chance of death, many would unhesitatingly opt for the potential magic bullet. The Declaration deals specifically with this situation (Article 35), although it hardly needs to do so. It says that the trial can be done. The other Articles, taken together, produce the same result. Mix informed consent with the principle that the inherent risks should be outweighed by the importance of the research, add the centrality of the individual research subject, and you've got Article 35. If the subject will die anyway if you don't give the magic bullet, the Declaration isn't offended if the magic bullet ends up going through the roof of the subject's mouth.

When should you stop?

You start your malaria study. The wonder drug works wonderfully—so wonderfully that it is very quickly clear that it's better than the competition. You're going to earn a lot of money from it, and so you're anxious to rush it onto the market. But too much rush is a bad idea. To annihilate the competition you want to continue the study for a little longer. Then the statistics buttressing your product will be unassailable.

But again, there's a problem. To continue the study in these circumstances might mean even more robust science (you'll prove your case to an extreme level of probability), but it also means more deaths. People in the control group will die in order to refine your scientific (and hence commercial) case. Is it worth it?

The Declaration (Article 20) demands that a study is stopped immediately when 'the risks are found to outweigh the potential benefits or when there is conclusive proof of positive and beneficial results'. This, of course, begs many questions. When, statistically, can one say that the risks outweigh the potential benefits? When does proof of a positive result become 'conclusive'? The Declaration gives no guidance. Presumably if this issue were to be litigated by people who had been harmed by or failed to benefit from a trial, it would turn on the relevant domestic law. Was it, for instance, *Bolam*-negligent to fail to stop the trial at a particular time? In theory such issues will have been decided in advance and built into the diligently vetted trial design. But it's not always so.

Children and incompetent adults

The spectre of experimentation on people who cannot validly give or refuse consent is terrifying. The Declaration seeks to exorcise it by tight controls. Such potential subjects cannot be used (my word, designed to raise Kantian hackles) in a research study that has no likelihood of benefiting them personally, unless it's intended to promote the health of the population from which the subject comes (say children, or adult patients with Down syndrome), the research can't be done with competent subjects, the study entails only minimal risk and burden, and informed consent has been obtained from the relevant proxy decision-maker, where one exists (Article 27).

What happens, though, where the test for lawful proxy consent is the 'best interests' of the individual patient, and there's no conceivable benefit to the individual subject? This is very common indeed. Take studies of normal child physiology, for instance. Typically blood samples will be taken. That poses only minimal risk, but it's uncomfortable, and confers no benefit whatever to the screaming child. To say that participation is in the child's best interests is to take an unfashionably wide, communitarian view of 'best interests'. The result has been massive under-testing of products for use in children. Many of the drugs used routinely in paediatric medicine are, for this reason, not specifically licensed for use in children. The studies that would be necessary to get the regulator's rubber stamp haven't been thought to be ethically or legally appropriate.

Payment

Everyone has seen adverts for medical research participants. Depending on the country, they might say 'Remuneration of expenses', or, more brazenly, 'Generous compensation for your time and trouble'. But everyone knows what's being offered. Money is given as an inducement to allow bodies to be experimented on. And people are induced.

The Declaration itself is silent about the payment of money to research subjects. It contents itself with saying that researchers must ensure that consent is real. There are many things that might taint the reality of consent. Money is one of them, says the orthodoxy. That orthodoxy is embodied in many local protocols, which typically insist that payment is restricted to the reimbursement of expenses and compensation for the time taken. Those protocols are ignored. The law, whose main concern is coercion of a darker kind, turns a Nelsonian blind eye. Across the world there's payment for participation. Research on healthy volunteers would stop if there weren't. There aren't enough genuine altruists out there, happy, just for the love of science and their fellow men, to give up their afternoons and their blood.

There's nothing offensive about this pragmatism. The relationship between money and voluntariness is too complex to be summarized in one or even many paragraphs of a code. Most people wouldn't go to work if they weren't paid, and yet rarely is it suggested that there should be laws to stop them working. Workers in dangerous occupations tend to get paid more: again it

is rarely suggested that compensation for risks is contrary to
public policy.

Project review and the outlawing of mavericks

The amateurish, ad hoc 'let's-start-it-and-see-how-it-goes'
maverick is dead. Or dead-ish. The Declaration has certainly done
its best to see him off. It seeks to entrench its own principles by
demanding that research is done systematically and thoughtfully,
with due regard to the ethical issues at stake. Its main entrenching
tool is the research ethics committee, to which a research protocol
must be submitted, by which the protocol must be approved, and
which has the right to monitor the progress of the research.

Each country has a slightly different way of arranging this
regulatory oversight. All too often the policemen of the ad hoc and
amateurish are ad hoc and amateurish themselves—sometimes
failing to understand the science they are supposed to be
regulating, sometimes too cavalier about the ethics. Perhaps the
real problem is a crisis of identity: they don't know what they are
meant to be. Are they meant to be the eyes and conscience of the
public? Or the guardian of the rights of the research subjects? Is
there a difference between these functions? How should the
interests of researchers and potential beneficiaries be
represented? Does a committee discharge its function if it goes
through a thorough, transparent, and consistent procedure, or is
there a notional 'right answer' to each problem it faces? There is
no consistency within nations, let alone worldwide, about these
central questions. It's not surprising that academic and political
observers of the committees haven't been deafening in their
applause.

Perhaps the most embattled committees are the Institutional
Review Boards (IRBs) in the US, and the most damaging
criticisms levelled against them are of conflicts of interest. Many
have spent a lot of time in bed with big pharmaceutical and

medical device manufacturers, and have come away with some nasty ethical diseases. A 2006 study of IRB members at university medical centres showed that over a third rarely or never disclosed their conflicts of interests to other members of the IRB, and over a third had financial ties to relevant industries. The US government has promised to clean up the IRBs. It remains to be seen how successful it is.

Chapter 8
Resource allocation

There is an infinite amount of suffering in the world. There is a distinctly finite amount of resources to deal with it. How do we decide who gets what? The dilemmas are agonizing. One man's treatment is another man's denial of treatment. To save X is to condemn Y.

Medical creativity has made the problem worse. If the options available to doctors were now what they were 100 years ago, we would stand a reasonable chance of being able to give everyone the treatment available. But so much more can now be done. Each new advance generates a new moral dilemma.

Each dilemma is politically explosive. Should life-saving and life-enhancing innovation be available only to the rich who can afford to pay for it themselves? If there's a state health service, should the government say frankly: 'We'll provide the basics. If you want anything exotic, you'd better go private'? Or should it say instead: 'We can't give everyone everything for free, but to show that we're true democrats, we'll give some patients the world-class, cutting-edge treatment'? But if so, which patients? And if the obligation is to provide the basics, what are those basics?

We tend to look at these problems through exclusively western, or at least narrowly national, eyes. About 40,000 children died today of hunger. Tens of thousands more died of malaria, and tens of thousands more of waterborne infectious diseases. Almost all of these were preventable. The money spent on a few heart transplants in elderly westerners would have saved almost all those lives.

Who'd get involved in all this if they could possibly help it? Well, not the judges. They've made that very clear. Wherever in the world an advocate stands up to suggest that health-care resources have been deployed unlawfully, there's a sharp intake of judicial breath, followed by the noise of Pilatian hand-washing. When the courts are pressed to give reasons for their non-intervention they come over all democratic, insisting that interfering with health-care resource allocation policy would be to usurp unacceptably the function of the legislature, or, where the question is whether a particular treatment should be provided to A rather than B, that this turns on clinical judgement, and accordingly it would be inappropriate to interfere.

They are not consistently deferential, of course. Legislative decisions are often pre-empted or struck down in the course of judicial review—usually by reference to a constitution or a set of human rights principles. And in many jurisdictions that bulwark of judicial deference to clinical opinion, the *Bolam* test, has been demolished or eroded. Judicial reluctance to say 'Yes' or 'No' to life-sustaining treatment has more to do with human reluctance to make hard decisions than with legal principle. Judges want to be able to sleep at night. And who can blame them?

The people who do blame them are the desperate litigants.

There are few more desperate than the parents of 10-year-old 'Child B'. She suffered from leukaemia. The prognosis didn't look good, but there was one possible treatment, which had a 20 per cent chance of success. The health authority refused to fund it,

and the parents challenged that refusal in the English Court of
Appeal. They failed. Unless the authority could be shown to have
acted irrationally in its decisions about resource allocation, the
court could not interfere (*R v Cambridge Health Authority ex p B*
(1995)).

That's how it works in most places in the world.

It's hard to be irrational. Most claims of irrationality in the arena
of health-care funding are framed not as an outright assault on
the outcome (such assaults are generally hopeless), but as attacks
on the decision-making process. Suppose that an authority
decides not to fund gender reassignment surgery for transsexuals.
If its reason is simply that it thinks it is more important to buy
kidney dialysis machines for the money that it would otherwise
spend on the surgery, the decision is likely to be unimpeachable.
But if the same decision is reached because the authority thinks

7. Patients in an African clinic wait for treatment. In every country
medical needs outstrip medical resources, creating agonizing
dilemmas about which the law has to take a view

that, as a matter of public policy, sex change ought to be discouraged, the outcome might be very different.

Discrimination itself isn't unlawful. It's essential. The law simply requires discrimination to be transparent and reasonable. In most jurisdictions, for instance, it wouldn't be unlawful to deny cardiac bypass surgery to smokers as long as the decision was justified carefully. The justification wouldn't be hard. The success rate for the surgery is significantly lower for smokers. Put another way (the utilitarian way beloved of hospital accountants), you get fewer Quality Adjusted Life Years per dollar when you spend your dollars on smokers. The surgery is not good value for money.

Human rights legislation has had surprisingly little impact on the law of health-care resource allocation. One might have thought that, in countries that apply the European Convention on Human Rights, Article 2 (which imposes a liability on states to institute measures to protect life), Article 3 (which prohibits inhuman and degrading treatment), and Article 8 (which, broadly, protects autonomy and gives people a qualified right to live their lives as they wish) might have made decisions about health-care funding rather more justiciable. But it hasn't happened.

Article 14 prohibits discrimination in the way that the other Convention rights are recognized or effected, but it's hard to point to a case where Article 14 would give a claimant a remedy but the domestic law would not. The transsexuals whose surgery had been denied on the basis of public policy would be able to frame their claim in terms of Article 14, but why bother? In most western countries discrimination of that sort is irrational and unlawful without Article 14's help. Some countries, of course, aren't so enlightened, and would endorse a public policy of discrimination. But although the Article 14 challenge might succeed against them in the European Court of Human Rights, the victory would be a pyrrhic one. The errant country would just be less candid in future about its reasons for denying the surgery.

So much for policymaking. What about decisions about individual patient care?

A patient in permanent vegetative state (PVS) lies on the ward, being fed through a nasogastric tube. If the diagnosis is right, by definition she does not get, and cannot ever get, anything at all out of life (although her family may get some comfort from visiting her). It's very expensive to keep her there. She might lie there for years. Her existence is killing and disabling lots of perfectly salvageable patients. She is, in particular, a lethal parasite on the patient in the bed next to her. That patient, a 35-year-old mother of four, has an entirely curable type of cancer. But the hospital doesn't have the money to pay for the necessary drugs.

Should one kill the PVS parasite (who many would say was really dead already) so that the mother can live? Well, perhaps. But the law in most jurisdictions—with a wary eye on the consequences of saying that one human life is worth more than another—will not say so. Indeed the UK House of Lords, in *Airedale NHS Trust v Bland* (1993), said that in deciding whether to withdraw life-sustaining treatment from the PVS patient, it was illegitimate to take into account the funds that would be released to treat others. Most other countries agree.

Let's examine that. It's lawful to have in place a policy that says that one will treat a class of patient with condition X, but not one with condition Y. It's lawful for the clinicians on the ward with the PVS and the cancer patient to decide on clinical grounds to maintain the PVS patient but not the cancer patient, or even to say to the cancer patient: 'Sorry. We've run out of money in this year's budget. You'll have to die.' If the cancer patient says to a court: 'It's irrational to condemn me and save the PVS patient,' she'll get short shrift. The court won't interfere.

Some judges are unhappy with this abdication of responsibility. Judges are, after all, paid to judge. They already make awesome decisions about the withdrawal of life-sustaining treatment; they sometimes (for instance in cases involving the separation of conjoined twins, where the separation will kill one but save the other) weigh one life against another (although they typically protest, unconvincingly, that that's not what they're doing). Hospital funding committees have to take decisions about whom to treat and whom to deny. They don't do that with the benefit of much more information or skill than a judge could, with the help of expert evidence, bring to bear on the same questions. Individual clinicians no doubt take financial considerations into account when deciding whether to treat X rather than Y—it's just that the law as it presently stands requires them to deny they're doing it. If clinicians can do it, why can't judges? And wouldn't it be healthier if clinicians were encouraged to be honest about the basis of their decisions?

The problem, of course, is not just a lack of judicial will or expertise. It's not, either, that it would be hard to devise a system of substantive law that did the job. The real problem is the old one of the floodgates. Make it too easy to challenge funding decisions, and the courts would be swamped by patients and their relatives scrabbling for the money. Very often the substantive law is shaped by practical considerations: health-care resource allocation is a classic example.

Chapter 9
The end of life

A terminally ill patient lies in a hospital bed. A doctor comes in and stands beside her bed. He draws the curtain around, so that no one can see what he's doing. He takes an instrument out of the bag he's holding. He does something to the patient using the instrument. Whatever he does causes the patient to die.

What should the law do?

The answer, of course, is that it depends on many, many things. Lots of crucial information is missing.

We'd need to know where the hospital was. If this is a case of euthanasia or assisted suicide, there are some juridictions where it would not be unlawful. If it was euthanasia, and took place somewhere where euthanasia was lawful, we'd need to know whether the procedures prescribed by the euthanasia law had been followed. Those procedures might include certification by independent practitioners that the patient was terminally ill within the meaning of the relevant law; that the patient had voluntarily requested euthanasia, having been fully informed of the prognostic and palliative facts; that there was no undue influence on the patient from relatives or carers; that there had been a 'cooling-off' period since the request for euthanasia; that the request was signed and duly witnessed; and so on.

We'd want to know what instrument the doctor used. If it was a syringe, and he'd given an injection that caused death, we'd want to know what was in the syringe. If it was potassium chloride, we'd probably want to call the police. A bolus of potassium chloride stops the heart immediately. It has no therapeutic use at all, unless you think that death is a type of healing. But even if the agent were potassium chloride, we couldn't immediately conclude that the doctor was guilty of murder (which is killing someone, intending to kill them or to cause them serious bodily harm). The doctor might have injected the drug thinking that it was something benign. In that case we'd be thinking about gross negligence manslaughter, and we'd have to ask questions such as: Did the doctor draw up the drug himself? And if so did he check the ampoule sufficiently carefully? (It sounds as if we'd have trouble establishing that.) Was he handed the syringe, ready filled, by a nurse? If so, does the law say that it's fine for him to assume that the nurse will have done her job properly, or is it grossly negligent (or merely negligent) to have delegated that duty? If the nurse handed him a syringe full of potassium chloride knowing that he would inject it into the patient with fatal consequences, is *she* guilty of murder?

If the syringe was full of morphine, some of the same questions would be asked, but there might, depending on the dose and the patient's condition and clinical history, be some others. The doctor might be able to take refuge in the doctrine of double effect, which distinguishes between intention and foresight, saying that if you do an action with intention A, but knowing that B might happen too, then you may be able to escape criminal liability for B.

Here, if the doctor injected morphine with the intention of relieving the patient's pain, but knowing that the dose required for proper pain relief might tip the patient into the grave, he would not be guilty of murder.

Perhaps, though, the instrument that the doctor took out of his bag was simply a pair of scissors. Perhaps he had used them to cut the tape around a tracheostomy tube that connected the patient to the ventilator that was keeping her alive. Perhaps the doctor had then removed the tube, causing the patient to die.

Those facts would generate a host of other questions. Some we've met already. This might be murder or gross negligence manslaughter. It may be, though, that the doctor might have been guilty of assault if he had *not* removed the tube. The patient might have been entirely mentally capacitous, and might have insisted on the removal. Or the patient might have been incapacitous, but she might have made a binding advance directive (living will), saying that if she got into the state that she was in when the doctor arrived, she wanted to refuse all life-sustaining treatment. It may be that the doctor was withdrawing the feeding tube that was keeping her unlawfully alive, or the catheter through which she was getting the antibiotics that were staving off the deadly bacteria that, were she capacitous, she would see as her merciful friends.

In short, death is a complicated business. Even saying what it is is difficult.

The definition of death

The heart of a hanged person sometimes continues to beat for 20 minutes after the plunge through the trapdoor. Some cells can continue to function for a long time after the body of which they are a part has ceased to ventilate them and pump blood. We all die slowly and incrementally.

Some injuries can wipe out a person's cerebral cortex. The person will never again be capable of pain, pleasure, communication, or any other sensation. Their relatives often talk about them as if they were dead. And yet the patient's heart will be beating and their chest rising and falling as they breathe unaided. Is there anything wrong about burying such a patient?

The law has two broad concerns. It wants to ensure that people are irrevocably dead before they are buried, cremated, or their vital organs are harvested for donation. And it wants to protect the sensibilities of relatives and friends. However biologically certain it is that a person will never recover, the traumatized family is unlikely to be happy about shovelling earth onto a heaving chest.

The brain stem—the evolutionarily ancient, vegetative part of the brain—contains, among other things, the respiratory centres which drive ventilation. If the brain stem is knocked out, not only is it immensely unlikely that there will be any higher cortical function (making many people unwilling to distinguish between brain-stem death and whole-brain death), but unaided respiratory function is also impossible. The heart may, however, continue beating for a while. If the patient is ventilated, it may continue to beat for a long time.

There are undoubted advantages in adopting a definition of death based only on demonstration of brain-stem death. It may mean, for instance, that organs can be taken from a patient when they are still being perfused by the patient's own beating heart, and when the organs are therefore in optimal condition for transplantation. It may mean that resources are not spent ventilating a patient who is certainly doomed and who has no conceivable interest in remaining, in a narrow, biological sense, alive.

These are the sort of considerations that have led the UK, amongst many other jurisdictions, to adopt a definition of death based on brain-stem death. The protocols to be followed in reaching the diagnosis of death are tightly controlled. They always involve demonstration of a patient's inability to breathe spontaneously, and may be supplemented by other investigations such as cerebral angiograms.

The difficulty with legislating in this area is that legislation has to cover all possible cases. We've already noted that the heart of a brain-stem-dead patient on a ventilator may beat happily for a long time. Legislators, therefore, have tended to hedge their bets. The US Uniform Determination of Death Act 1980 provides, for instance, that a dead person is one who has sustained irreversible cessation of either 'circulatory and respiratory function' or 'all functions of the entire brain, including the brain stem'.

Deadly acts and deadly omissions

At the heart of much legal thinking about death and dying is the distinction between acts and omissions.

Tony Bland was crushed in a football stadium. Much of his cerebral cortex was wiped out. He went into a persistent vegetative state (PVS). He was insensate, and always would be. He knew nothing of the devoted relatives who, for years, came to sit beside him in hospital. His heart worked, he could breathe, and he had a functioning gut. But that was about the limit of his life. He was kept alive by being fed and hydrated through a tube.

Eventually his family decided that enough was enough. It was time to acknowledge that the Tony they loved had gone. His doctors agreed. The best way to deal with this, they all decided, was to withdraw his feeding tube. Deprived of food and fluids he would soon be dead. By definition, if the diagnosis of PVS was right, he would have no idea what was happening to him.

But there was a problem. If the withdrawal of food and fluids amounted to an act, it would be an act done with the intention of causing death. If it in fact caused death, his doctors would be guilty of murder. If, instead of pulling out a feeding tube, they, with identical intent, pressed the plunger of a syringe containing a lethal drug, they would certainly be guilty of murder. What was the difference?

The difference, said the UK House of Lords (*Airedale NHS Trust v Bland* (1993)), was that the withdrawal of food and fluids was an omission.

This has caused lots of brow-furrowing. It doesn't take much legal sleight of hand to transform an act into an omission and vice versa. If I starve a child to death by refusing to feed it, I should expect a frosty reception to my submission at my murder trial that I was only omitting to do something. And there are various thought experiments devised by philosophers that seek to indicate that there is no distinction of substance between acts and omissions. Perhaps the most famous is the 'Trolley problem': perhaps the most accessible is the story of the two wicked uncles.

Uncle A stands to gain a huge inheritance if baby C dies. He offers to bath the baby. He pushes its head under the water. It drowns. He is guilty of murder.

Uncle B, too, will be massively enriched by baby C's death. He too gives the baby its bath. Just as he is reaching out his hand to push C's head beneath the water, C accidentally knocks her own head on the side of the bath and sinks beneath the water. It would require no effort at all for B to raise C's head and save her. But of course he's delighted by this windfall. He stands and watches, rubbing his avaricious hands, as C drowns.

In most jurisdictions B will have committed no criminal offence at all. A few jurisdictions impose a duty of rescue in these circumstances, but they don't regard failure to rescue as murder. And yet the action of Uncle A is ethically identical to the omission of Uncle B. Isn't the law being absurd in failing to acknowledge it?

Well, possibly. But many feel that, however many anomalies can be pointed out by imaginative philosophers, there is a distinction of great emotional weight and intellectual utility between acts and omissions. One of the uses was demonstrated in *Bland*:

well-meaning doctors don't get locked up for refusing to continue pointless treatment.

Murder, euthanasia, and assisted suicide

If you went into a bar and injected a fatal dose of a drug into someone, intending to kill them or to do them really serious harm, you'd be guilty, wherever you were in the world, of murder. Note, importantly, that motive and intention are different. Many people commit murders with compassionate motives. The classic example is the 'mercy killer' who, wishing to spare his wife more agony, puts a pillow over her face and suffocates her. His motives are love and mercy: his intention is to kill.

Lilian Boyes suffered for many years from rheumatoid arthritis. It became increasingly agonizing. She howled like a dog when she was touched. Palliative options were exhausted. She repeatedly begged her physician, Dr Cox, to put her out of her misery. He repeatedly refused. There were no doubts about her mental capacity. She continued to beg and to howl. At last Dr Cox gave her a lethal injection. He wrote up in her medical notes what he had done. A nurse contacted the police, and Dr Cox was tried for attempted murder (an attempt rather than the completed offence, notionally because the prosecution could not prove definitively that the injection was the cause of the death—it was theoretically possible that she had died of an entirely unrelated arrhythmia just as the plunger was pressed—but more likely because the prosecution realized that a jury would be more likely to convict of attempted murder since a murder conviction carries a mandatory life sentence in the UK). The case was indefensible. The law was clear. He was legally indistinguishable from the husband with the pillow, and was duly convicted. His benign motive was reflected in his sentence—a short and wholly suspended sentence of imprisonment: see *R v Cox* (1992).

All of us surely have sympathy both for Lilian Boyes and for Dr Cox. The question is whether that sympathy is a good reason for a change in the law of murder.

Proponents of the legalization of euthanasia tend to use two strands of argument. First, they contend that compassion makes euthanasia morally mandatory. We wouldn't let our dog continue to scream for years with uncontrolled pain: we'd take it to the vet to be put down. Why should we deny to humans what basic decency makes us do to our dogs? And second, they emphasize autonomy. Our lives are our own, they say. We can decide what to do with them. If we choose to end them, that's our business.

The opponents of a change in the law are often, but by no means always, motivated by a belief in the sanctity of life which is often rooted in the notion of the Imago Dei—the idea that God's image is stamped on all humans, and that to take life is to efface that image. They are typically suspicious about the primacy of autonomy, suggesting that it is not the only principle in play. They note that the exercise of X's autonomy necessarily affects the life (and the exercise of the autonomy) of Y. A special and important example of this is the asserted slippery slope from voluntary euthanasia to involuntary euthanasia (the killing of a patient who has not consented to it, or not consented to it when in possession of all the relevant facts, or who has consented to it under some sort of duress from relatives or carers, or who simply feels that their continued existence is a burden to others).

Whether this slippery slope exists in jurisdictions where euthanasia is lawful, and if so whether any block can be placed on it to stop practice sliding disastrously all the way down to the bottom, are matters of intense debate. It is probably true that capacity-truncating depression is a common and under-diagnosed condition in patients who ask for euthanasia. This means that there is reason to wonder about the validity of the consent they give, and reason to wonder whether, if their depression were treated, the desire for death would recede. But it does not necessarily mean that no sufficient safeguards can be put in place to relegate these concerns to the status of mere slogan.

If autonomy is the sole arbiter of action, say the opponents of euthanasia, why restrict the right to die to terminally ill patients (as is usually the case in those jurisdictions where euthanasia is permissible)? Why not allow a tired, bored person to drop in at a euthanasia booth on the way home? They assume, in this argument, that this will be unthinkable.

The proponents of euthanasia have three responses. First, and most radically: 'Why not indeed? But sadly society's not yet mature enough for such a dramatically enlightened step.' Second, and often bolted on to the first: 'That's not the law we're asking for at the moment, so don't introduce irrelevancies.' And third, and more disarmingly: 'There may be real concerns about whether a request from a physically well person is made with full capacity. Autonomy would therefore be suspicious of the booth.'

Another argument from the opponents is based on the role of doctors, who would be doing the killing. If we say for the sake of argument that X has a right to be killed when, where, and in the circumstances that they wish, should that imply that X can say to Y: 'You must kill me, whether you want to or not?' If Y is society, perhaps this demand is not so offensive. If Y is a person, or perhaps even a profession, it becomes more tricky. And ultimately it is a profession, and a person within a profession, who has to do the killing.

Individual doctors, whatever their broader views on euthanasia, have tended to express distaste for doing the killing themselves. The medical profession in many countries, concerned about what euthanasia laws would do for the doctor–patient relationship, has been slow to endorse those laws. But this is not always the case: it is hard to make useful generalizations, particularly since so few countries have experience of euthanasia.

Significantly absent from the ranks of pro-euthanasia doctors are palliative-care physicians—those who deal with the reduction of pain and distress at the end of life. Their stance has tended to be that euthanasia is never necessary: that modern palliative care enables a good death for all. Even in the very rare cases where satisfactory analgesia is impossible, one can always sedate to unconsciousness—effectively anaesthetizing the patient until she dies.

The pro-euthanasists respond that good palliative care isn't available to everyone, and that it is absurd and intellectually dishonest to say that there's an ethical difference between ablating someone's consciousness permanently by anaesthesia and ablating it permanently by causing their death.

And so it rumbles on.

Assisted suicide is a close ally of euthanasia. But there are some important differences.

Most jurisdictions do not now make it an offence for a person to attempt to commit suicide. There are compelling reasons for this. Pressure for change came from doctors who noted that being the principal prosecution witness against a patient they had successfully pumped out was unlikely to help the therapeutic relationship with that patient. Often, however (for instance in the UK and many US states), it is an offence for someone to help someone commit suicide.

Assisting suicide of course covers a multitude of legal sins. Some are downright evil. Take, for instance, a recent UK case where the defendant persuaded his girlfriend that she was worthless, demon-possessed, and better off dead. She eventually believed him, drank the bottle of vodka he'd handed her to give her Dutch

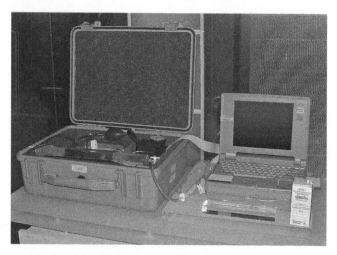

8. Philip Nitschke's 'Deliverance machine', once used legally in the Northern Territories of Australia. If the patient answered correctly a series of questions posed by a computer, a lethal dose of barbiturates was automatically injected

courage, and, at his encouragement, jumped off a bridge. Some are motivated simply by compassion. Some sort of legal control of assisted suicide seems appropriate, but so does a good deal of prosecutorial discretion.

Any sensible law permitting assisted suicide will, as all jurisdictions that have such laws recognize, need robust safeguards to ensure that requests for suicide are made voluntarily, without coercion, and in full knowledge and understanding of the relevant facts.

Withholding and withdrawing life-sustaining treatment

Ms B had a bleed into her cervical spinal cord. It paralysed her from the neck down. She couldn't breathe for herself: a ventilator had to do it for her.

She found her life unbearable. She asked her clinicians to turn off the ventilator and let her die. They refused. They were very fond of her, and they thought her life was worth living.

She took them to court, asking the court for an order that her continued ventilation was unlawful.

The only issue for the court was whether she was mentally competent to make the decision—whether she had the cognitive apparatus to understand what she was asking for—and whether she was properly informed. She was competent, and so the ventilation constituted an assault. The UK NHS body in charge of her care (as opposed to the doctors who had expressed their reluctance) was ordered to stop the ventilator and let her die: *B v An NHS Trust* (2002).

This was not a suicide or an act of euthanasia. It was a natural death. What killed Ms B was not the flick of the ventilator switch, but the bleed and the consequential respiratory paralysis. The case illustrates a principle respected in all jurisdictions: competent adults can decline even life-sustaining treatment. The alternative would be a frightening paternalism. For US examples, see *Satz v Perlmutter* (1978), *McKay v Bergstedt* (1990), and *Georgia v McAfee* (1989).

It is much more difficult with incapacitous patients.

A 45-year-old man is involved in a catastrophic accident. Like Tony Bland, he is in PVS. He has no sensation, nor will he ever have again, but he normally needs no active medical care other than tube feeding. He gets a chest infection. A five-day course of oral antibiotics would cure it. If it is not treated it will kill him. What should be done?

There are four common legal strategies.

Substituted judgement

Here, the decision-maker seeks to make the same judgement that have been made by the incapacitous patient were that patient not incapacitous. This will involve an inquiry into the patient's wishes and values.

This is a common approach in the US, but many states have recourse to the best interests strategy if the views of the patient cannot be determined with sufficient certainty.

The substituted judgement approach sounds good: its rhetoric is straightforward patient autonomy. But patients' supposed views are often inaccessible, or can be determined only by looking through the possibly jaundiced eyes of those, such as relatives or carers, who may have a stake in the patient's death. Few of us are articulately philosophical when it comes to considering how we'd like to die, and even fewer of us have the medical knowledge necessary to tailor our utterances closely to the clinical circumstances in which we are likely to approach death. There are, too, plenty of studies showing that, when we find ourselves in the medical situation that, when healthy, we feared most terribly, we find our lives much more valuable and bearable than we thought we would. I doubt that most of us factor that literature into those depressing end-of-life conversations we have in the early hours—precisely the sort of conversations that are likely to take centre stage in a determination of substituted judgement.

Substituted judgement, of course, can have no place in making decisions on behalf of people who have never been able to make or express decisions on their own behalf (for instance children or people who have never had capacity). Since most of us are more or less incompetent and inarticulate, and do not record our views reliably, it seems strange to say that there's such a rigid division between the technically incompetent and others that a wholly different test should be applied to each.

Best interests

The test used, for example, in the UK, is the best interests test, whereby an action or inaction will be lawful if it is in the best interests of the patient. 'Best interests' are considered holistically: they are not a mere audit of the 'medical best interests'.

In theory this is an objective test: something either is or is not, as a matter of fact, in someone's best interests.

In PVS cases judges have struggled (notoriously in *Bland*) with the question of whether a permanently, irretrievably unconscious patient has any interests at all, but surely such a patient does: he would want, for instance, to be remembered well. A PVS patient is not a mere piece of meat on a slab. Suppose it were proposed that medical students practised rectal examinations on a PVS patient. Would that be right? It would not, and that is because the patient has residual interests (perhaps best described as dignity interests, protected in Europe under, I suggest, Articles 8 and/or 3 of the European Convention on Human Rights) which can still be violated. You don't have to be cognate to be human or to be abused.

In practice, best interests determinations are often infused with substituted judgement. The English Mental Capacity Act 2005, for instance, requires a decision-maker to consider, when deciding where someone's best interests lie, any previous expressions of opinion by the patient. It's assumed, therefore, that it may not be in the best interests of a patient to be dealt with in a way with which they've previously indicated they'd be unhappy.

The courts often encourage a 'balance sheet' approach. They conduct an audit of the patient's life, listing in one column the factors in favour of continued existence, and in the other the factors in favour of death. Obviously not all factors have the same weight: judgement has to be applied. But once the factors are appropriately weighted, one theoretically adds up each column. The column with the highest score wins, and the judicial thumb is turned up or down accordingly.

This sounds easier and more scientific than it is. 'Best interests' are notoriously elusive. Sometimes (and particularly where the patient is very young and very disabled—perhaps even unable to manifest, by vocalization or facial expression, signs of pain or pleasure), it may be necessary for the law to make certain presumptions. One important presumption is the presumption in favour of continued existence. If you choose, you can call it a foundational respect for the sanctity of life. It has a long and distinguished lineage. It is crucially important in deciding how the various factors in the best interests audit are weighted. It is often decisive. But it can be (and often is) displaced.

Proxy decision-making

Sometimes people appoint someone to make decisions for them. This is typically done by a durable or lasting power of attorney. Often (for instance in many US states and in the UK), a power of attorney entitling the attorney to decline even life-saving or life-sustaining treatment on behalf of a patient has to comply with particular formalities that may not apply to more general powers of attorney.

Parents typically make proxy decisions for their children, of course. And that includes treatment decisions. But parental views are best regarded as an aid to determining where the child's best interests lie. They're a very helpful aid: so helpful, indeed, that they are presumed to be definitive of those best interests in most jurisdictions. But the presumption can be rebutted. The court has the last word.

It's broadly the same for proxy decision-making on behalf of adults. All the legislation that permits lasting powers of attorney reserves to the court the ability to review an attorney's decision. So the fate

9. The blind and the crippled call out for death: detail from Andrea Orcagna's *The Triumph of Death*. Death is not always seen as an unwelcome predator

of a person who has executed a power of attorney may nonetheless be decided according to (depending on the jurisdiction) the best interests or the substituted judgement test.

Advance directives

Otherwise known as 'living wills', these are expressions by a person made, when they are still competent, about how they would like to be treated when they are no longer competent. They may apply to the withdrawal or withholding of life-sustaining treatment, but particular formalities are often required when they do. They may take the form either of a statement of principles that the person would like to have applied in relation to their end-of-life decision-making, or of a medically specific direction such as: 'If I become mentally incapacitous and doubly incontinent I do not want any life-sustaining treatment.'

Their legal effect varies between jurisdictions. In some places they are merely evidence which can be taken into account in deciding what to do. In others they have the same effect, if valid and applicable, as a refusal by a competent patient.

Importantly they are almost always *refusals*. That's because it is very unusual to be able to compel a doctor actively to do something she's unhappy about. But stopping her doing something that she might consider worthwhile is very different.

They can be useful, but they need to be approached cautiously. They need to be kept updated. Medical science moves on, and patients' views change. By the time an advance directive becomes relevant, the therapeutic or palliative options, or the patient's personal circumstances or philosophical convictions might be very different from those that pertained when the directive was made.

Sometimes, too, disease can transform personality. Suppose X is terrified of Alzheimer's disease. He makes a directive saying that if he gets the disease he refuses life-sustaining treatment. His fears are realized. He is diagnosed with Alzheimer's dementia. It strips away a lot of his cortex, but it also strips from him much of the angst that, when he was capacitous, made his life hell. He seems to have been transported into a child-like Eden. He laughs with the nurses, giggles happily with his fellow patients, and watches, with apparent enjoyment, the very worst daytime TV. So far as anyone can tell he's happier than he's ever been.

But then he contracts a chest infection. Just as in the case of our 45-year-old road traffic victim, it will kill him in five days if it's not treated with oral antibiotics. The daughter, who is the sole beneficiary under his will, produces the advance directive, saying that if he is given the antibiotics she will sue for assault.

What should the doctors do? Doesn't it seem as if X has died, and that a different person, Y, has risen from his ashes? There's only a superficial biological continuity between X and Y. They share some cells. Why should a document signed by X, who is dead, be the warrant of execution of another person, Y, whom X never met and whose condition X never anticipated?

There is no straightforward answer to this question from any jurisdiction, although textbooks often suggest that there's nothing here to discuss—and that the death of Y is legally inevitable.

Withdrawing and withholding: no distinction

A final point: it's usual for lawyers and ethicists to assert that there's no material distinction between withdrawing and withholding treatment. The reason for that is clear enough. If there were a distinction, it might prove legally or ethically hard to stop treatment that had been started. That might make doctors reluctant to start potentially valuable treatment. And that would be in no one's interests.

Chapter 10

Organ donation and the ownership of body parts

At least if I'm in England, I don't own my own body. Indeed it is incapable of being owned. I don't even possess it: *R v Bentham* (2005).

This might seem odd. I feel and talk as if I own it. But when I feel and talk that way I'm being legally very sloppy. What I'm really saying is that I have a right (or at least more of a right than anyone else) to control what happens to my body. And if the proposition is put like that, the law agrees with me. Indeed, as we've seen when we looked at the law of consent, the law agrees very robustly indeed—as long as you're a legally competent adult who's in a hospital rather than in a sadomasochistic salon.

But the law has a problem with the notion of the living body as property. Yes, there's a problem with the dead body too, of ancient origins, but this is really a corollary of the problem with the living body. Why should my descendants have a claim to my corpse when I have no claim, when alive, to the same mass of cells?

The law's distaste has two roots. The first is theological. The law was framed by believers who thought that to assert ownership over oneself was blasphemous. We didn't create ourselves, and so we don't possess title over ourselves. This attitude (perhaps buttressed by a deeply entrenched instinct) persists, although the beliefs, by and large, do not. The second is related to it, but is a creature of Kant and the Enlightenment. It's a hatred of commodification.

'Distaste'; 'instinct'; 'hatred': these words sound anomalous in a book about the law. But in this area, perhaps more than any other (which is saying a lot), judges shoot from the intuitive hip. It's hard to trace consistent strands of reasoning: policy is dressed up, often very implausibly, as logic.

Now it's property, now it's not

But it's hard to get away completely from the notion of property. Property thinking and property language are sometimes very useful. And, by and large, the courts haven't bothered to get away. They have been messily pragmatic. To the extent to which it's convenient to see body parts as property, they have done so (peppering their judgments with caveats). The overall result has been that body parts are sometimes, sort of, property, and sometimes, most emphatically, they're not.

Here's an example of that pragmatism. The English Court of Appeal in *R v Kelly* (1999) reaffirmed the old, basic rule that there was no property in unmodified body parts. It went on: 'It may be that...on some future occasion...the courts will hold that human body parts are capable of being property for the purposes of [theft], even without the acquisition of different attributes, if they have a use or significance beyond their mere existence. This may be so if, for example, they are intended for use in an organ transplant operation, for the extraction of DNA, or...as an exhibit in a trial.' This is remarkable judicial frankness. It's saying, in effect: we'll invest something with whatever attributes it needs to have in order for us to do the Right Thing. That's no bad thing. Getting the right result is rather important. Its importance tends to be underrated by legal scholars.

The Germans are unusual in being forthright and consistent about the status of severed body parts. For the Germans, these are property. Most other jurisdictions try to find ways to avoid the simple, unequivocal label 'property' and its consequences.

The High Court of Australia is typical. Clinging, in *Doodeward v Spence* (1908), to the historical insistence that there was no property in a corpse (grave robbers were charged with theft of the shroud, or with obscure ecclesiastical offences concerning grave desecration), it said that someone who puts work or skill into the treatment of a dead body or a body part so that it acquires 'some attributes differentiating it from a mere corpse awaiting burial' acquires a right to retain possession.

Doodeward was the nemesis of the thieves who stole body parts from the Royal College of Surgeons. They argued that they could not be convicted of theft, since no property had been taken. Not so, said the English Court of Appeal. The parts had been preserved: labour had been expended on them. Accordingly they were sufficiently 'property' to be stolen: *R v Kelly* (1999).

Cases about the ownership of parts or products of a living human body have tested the judges' ability to get by without the notion of property.

In *Moore v Regents of the University of California* (1990) (Supreme Court of California), the claimant had leukaemia. His spleen and other body parts were removed and, without his consent, cells were used to establish a very economically and medically valuable cell line. The cell line was patented. It earned a lot of money, but not for the claimant.

He sued, contending, amongst other things, that his cells were property which had been 'converted' to the use of another. The court disagreed with this, concerned about the stifling effect on research that might result if entirely innocent researchers might be liable in conversion for working in good faith on a cell line of whose provenance they knew nothing. There were other remedies available to the claimant: the doctor who had removed the tissue without consent was liable for breach of fiduciary duty and for operating without consent. But those claims weren't worth anything like the billions of dollars represented by the cell line.

In *Hecht v Superior Court for Los Angeles County* (1993) (California Court of Appeals), semen could be property for the purposes of being disposed of under a will because the man who had ejaculated it had had sufficient decision-making authority in relation to that semen. It was that authority that rendered it property. The effect of this was that his girlfriend could recover the semen and use it for the purpose for which it had been ejaculated—namely to inseminate her. (Similar cases in England, such as *R v Human Fertilisation and Embryology Authority ex p Blood* (1999) and *Evans v Amicus Healthcare* (2004), are best seen as cases about reproductive autonomy and specific questions of statutory construction: they are considered in Chapter 3).

Policy, rather than legal logic, is behind both these decisions. In *Moore* it was thought that a property analysis would do, on balance, more harm than good, and so it was rejected. In *Hecht* it would do more good than harm, and so it was adopted.

In the English Court of Appeal case of *Yearworth v North Bristol NHS Trust* (2010), semen ejaculated for the purposes of conceiving children after chemotherapy for cancer was negligently destroyed. A wrong had clearly been done, but how should it be described? It was held that, although a statute restricted the use that the men could make of the semen, that restriction did not mean that they could not 'have ownership' of it for the purposes of a claim in negligence, and that accordingly 'it follows a fortiori that the men had sufficient rights in relation to it as to render them capable of having been bailors of it'. Both ownership and bailment (looking after a chattel) imply the recognition in that semen of some sort of property.

So, in the US, England, and elsewhere, body parts and the products of bodies are regarded as property if that gives the right answer.

What about trading in body parts, or things that my body produces? There's a market for human blood, for instance. Can I turn myself into a blood farm, milking myself of blood for profit? Selling one kidney could go a long way towards paying off my mortgage, and could well save someone's life.

If my blood and my kidney are my property, why not? Indeed, why should the lawfulness of the sales turn on the arcane and, as we've seen, rather arbitrary question of whether the label 'property' should be applied to each? Even if my kidney isn't property, and I have no right to possess it in the sense understood by land lawyers, I've still got much more right than anyone else to decide what happens to it. If I choose to wreck my kidneys by marinating them each night in gin, the law won't stop me. Why should it stop me doing something financially sensible and socially useful? A prostitute in many jurisdictions can lawfully sell her body for sex. Why should she not sell her blood for the manufacture of life-saving blood products?

The knee-jerk ethical answer, of course, is 'commodification'—an answer that begs endless questions. Yes, this is commodification, but so what? A proper answer perhaps has to deploy the language of human dignity.

Many jurisdictions have prohibited commercial dealings in human organs and body products. The general international tone is heard in Article 21 of the Council of Europe's Convention on Human Rights and Biomedicine (1997), which provides that: 'The human body and its parts shall not, as such, give rise to financial gain.'

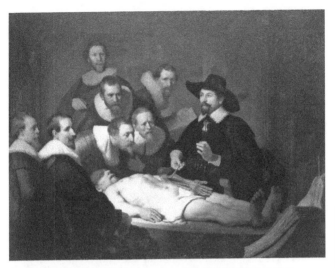

10. Rembrandt's *The Anatomy Lesson of Professor Nicolaes Tulp*. Should you have an absolute right to determine what happens to your body after your death?

Organ donation

The demand for organs massively exceeds supply.

One solution, in relation to some organs, such as kidneys, is to encourage donation by living people. That is discussed briefly above. Altruistic donation of, for instance, bone marrow or even a kidney by live donors is lawful in many jurisdictions, often, and particularly in the case of a significant sacrifice such as a kidney, after an extensive investigation by a regulatory body to check that the would-be donor is making the offer freely, and understands fully what is involved. But this obviously won't work for hearts, lungs, and so on. If they are to be used at all, they have to be retrieved from dead bodies.

There are two main legal worries about this. The first concerns consent: have the deceased or, where appropriate, the relatives, given the appropriate permission? And the second concerns death: is the deceased really, irretrievably dead?

The ability of people to decide what happens to their bodies after their deaths is, in most countries, largely governed by statute. Those statutes generally tend to assume that autonomy extends into the grave, and that we should each be able to decide whether we rot, burn, or are recycled.

Several mechanisms are used to honour autonomy. Some jurisdictions say that if you haven't indicated what you want done with your body, it is wrong to use any organs. One therefore has to 'opt in' to donation. Others assume that if you had any objection to donation, you'd have said so, and accordingly that silence indicates consent: ('opt out'). Others require you to make a choice, for instance as a requirement of obtaining a driving licence ('mandated choice'). There is a great deal of discussion among ethicists about the acceptability of these options, and among politicians and doctors about their efficacy in increasing donation rates, but they are legally not very interesting.

More legally interesting are the questions that concern the definition of death (discussed in Chapter 9) (on which turns the propriety of harvesting organs from 'beating-heart donors') and the suggestions that are sometimes made about taking organs from patients in permanent vegetative state (universally unlawful at the moment, on precisely the same grounds as it would be unlawful to remove organs from a healthy person who happens to be undergoing an anaesthetic for an appendectomy) and from anencephalic children (which turns in all countries, at the moment, on satisfaction of the standard criteria for determining death, but which one might coherently argue should be more readily done, since the prognosis is so obvious and so dire).

Guidelines from the World Health Organization embody the broad international consensus on the safeguards to be applied when it is proposed to remove organs from a beating-heart donor, including—for ghoulishly obvious reasons—a requirement that death is certified by someone other than the clinicians who want to effect the transplant.

Intellectual property rights

The idea that a biotechnology company should point to a piece of the genome and say 'That's mine: I alone have the right to make money from knowledge of the sequence' raises all sorts of political, philosophical, and theological hackles.

As one might expect from the case of *Moore* (above), the Americans are more laissez-faire about this than the Europeans. Their deep-seated free-market tendencies, in this respect at least, get the better of their religious conservatism. The Supreme Court, endorsing a patent for a genetically engineered oil-eating bacterium, observed that the legislature had intended the patent laws to include 'anything under the sun that is made by man', and that 'made by man', in this context, included the manipulation by man of naturally occurring nucleic acid: *Diamond v Chakrabarty* (1980).

The difference between the US and Europe was shown clearly by a mouse. Harvard University produced a mouse (the OncoMouse), which was a sort of biological time bomb. It had a human cancer gene stitched into its DNA, so that it inevitably developed cancer. Harvard patented the mouse without any problem in the US. But the Europeans were more cautious. The mouse eventually got its patent, but not without a struggle against the contentions that it was immoral to patent a living organism and unlawful to patent an animal variety (both objections that arose out of the European Patent Convention).

For fewer patents for human gene sequences have been granted in Europe, than in the US. But for a time it seemed that Europe was easing up. DNA, it has been held in Europe, is not 'life', and accordingly the 'playing God'-type objections fall away. It would be disastrous for research funding, it was said, were it otherwise. But the Europeans remain intrinsically conservative when it comes to the patentability of human material. That conservatism is now embodied in the 1998 EC Directive on the patentability of biotechnological inventions. It indicates clearly where the battle lines for future legal and ethical debate are drawn. Article 5(1) provides that 'The human body, at the various stages of its formation and development, and the simple discovery of one of its elements, including the sequence or partial sequence of a gene, cannot constitute patentable inventions.' And, by Article 6(1), '[I]nventions shall be considered unpatentable where their commercial exploitation would be contrary to *ordre public* or morality...the following, in particular, shall be considered unpatentable:...processes for cloning human beings... [and]...uses of human embryos for industrial or commercial purposes.' The general position of those battle lines is similar in most jurisdictions.

Confidentiality: where the body tells a story

A celebrity stays in a hotel. The chambermaid scrapes the flakes of dandruff off the pillow and sells them to a national newspaper, which proposes to analyse the DNA with a view to saying whether or not the celebrity is the father of a much discussed lovechild. Can the celebrity say that the dandruff is his property and should be returned to him? Is it property at all? If it is, has the celebrity abandoned it, so that anyone who picks it up acquires title in it?

The example isn't so far from the real world of medical law. In the storerooms of many hospitals across the world there are tissues, legitimately removed in the course of operations and autopsies, which have been retained without the explicit consent of their erstwhile 'owners'. They too can disclose valuable information— valuable to medical researchers, but potentially valuable too to insurance companies, who might be able to tell from scanning the genome whether the person from whom the tissue was claimed is a good insurance risk.

The dandruff and the hospital storeroom cases are very similar. The storeroom sample is bigger, which hardly seems like a sound reason for treating it in a different way from the dandruff. And yet, largely because of the sample size, lawyers across the world are much more ready to worry about whether the storeroom sample amounts to property and should be treated as property than they are about the dandruff.

We've seen already some of the problems about viewing body parts, whether of the living or the dead, as property. We've seen that the law is pragmatically happy to dub something property if that helps to give the right answer. But in both these cases, there's really no need to begin to use property language to protect the interests that need protecting. What's important is not the tissue itself, but the information that it bears. The best analysis is in the law of confidentiality or privacy, not of property.

Lawyers and legislators in many jurisdictions are slowly realizing this. In the UK Human Tissue Act 2004, for instance, the unauthorized analysis of DNA is specifically recognized as a mischief in its own right. That's surely the way forward—tailoring the remedy to the harm, rather than squeezing the problem into artificial and archaic boxes (such as the 'property' box), so complicating and distorting the law.

Chapter 11
The future of medical law

Medical law, as a distinct speciality, is young. But young, in the law, doesn't necessarily mean fit. And the medical law needs to be fit to keep up with the dramatically fast-moving professions it seeks to regulate.

How is that fitness best achieved? Should we rip up the rag-tag, piecemeal, ad hoc collection of principles, rules, and speculations that comprise medical law, complaining that they're irredeemably contaminated with Victorian notions of contract, duty, and trust, and draft a brand new, up-to-the-minute code, informed by neuroscientific understandings of human volition and purged of metaphysics?

I suggest that we muddle on: that we evolve rather than revolt. The subject matter of medical law has always been and will always be the same: humans. The law that we've got was devised for humans by clever, reflective humans. The new problems that we'll get will be variations of old problems. You can't safely purge metaphysics from the law because you can't purge the metaphysics from humans.

But the speed of evolution needs to increase. Lawyers need to become more medically and philosophically literate. Good law presupposes a good understanding both of the medical facts and of the philosophical repercussions. That's a big brief. The proliferation of medical law and ethics texts and courses suggests that it can be mastered. In Chapter 1 we looked at the complex relationship between law and ethics. But in the end the nature of the relationship doesn't matter so much, as long as it's close and amicable. The conversation between the two is ever more vital.

Medicine is becoming increasingly technical, evidence-based, and protocol-driven. Despite a desperate rearguard action by the advocates of medical humanities, it's increasingly embarrassing to talk about the Art of medicine. Talk about the death of the Art becomes a self-fulfilling prophecy. The medicine of the future will be run by technically brilliant nerds. They'll look at their screens, or their shoes, but never at the patient, let alone at Sophocles. They haven't got the time, even if they had the inclination or the ability, to wonder about whether a particularly sexy new intervention is dehumanizing. And if they concluded that it was, they might think that that was not a contraindication at all.

It's therefore very important that medical law isn't over-deferential to medicine, as it has tended to be. *Bolam* should be nudged towards extinction, or at least put on the back foot, not because medicine is increasingly the business of accurately following a definitive guideline (which is the threat to *Bolam* at the moment), but because the law, not the doctors, should set the law's standards. Law has the opportunity and the duty to be appropriately holistic. Medicine has the duty, but has just about lost the opportunity.

It needs confident medical lawyers to do law's job properly. Some of *Bolam*'s more extravagant abuses arose simply because the advocates and the judges didn't have the first idea what the doctors were talking about, and so decided that they ought to give the defendant the benefit of the doubt. There would have been no doubt in the minds of better-educated judges. So we should have specialist judges. They will be faster, more medically fluent, and (at least because they're not thumbing, intimidated, through a medical dictionary during the lunchtime adjournment) will have more chance of becoming properly steeped in the wider literature—the literature that will allow them to take the wide, deep, and long view that medicine has denied itself.

There are dangers with having a professional medical judiciary. It might attract the brothers of the medical nerds. It might mean that medical law is denied the cross-fertilization from other legal disciplines that has proved so fecund in the past. It doesn't matter so much if a commercial court judge is simply a bewigged brain on a stick: he's just got to deal with money. Medical judges have to deal with bodies, minds, and souls, and with whatever strange glue sticks them together. An interest in the mechanics of bodies might denote a lack of interest in the mechanics of souls. That would be sad. But, by and large, expert medical judges are a risk worth taking. We've already got, in many jurisdictions, a cadre of expert medical lawyers. They are made of good stuff.

They need to be. There are some intellectually epic challenges ahead.

What's the status of the human embryo? Is it equivalent for all purposes (and if not, why?) to the adult? Is it ever permissible to kill X to save Y? If not, what should you do with the patient in PVS whose continued existence is consuming the funds that would buy life-saving treatment for many? Suppose the money spent on a cosmetic breast enlargement operation in London would save the lives of 10,000 children in the Congo. Should a judge in a London court conclude that it's rational to enlarge the London breasts? Is life legally an all-or-nothing thing? Does a patient who hovers in the no-man's-land between unconsciousness and death have precisely the same rights as a fully alert and healthy child? Does a woman have a right to inseminate herself with the semen left in a condom her boyfriend and she have just used? If so, what are the consequences for the boyfriend? Is it lawful to remove surgically the healthy legs of a patient because she decides she wants them mounted as an exhibit in her bathroom? A deaf couple, wanting to have a child with whom they can share the intimacy of the deaf world, create embryos by way of IVF, screen the embryos for a 'deaf' gene, and implant a 'deaf' embryo into the mother's uterus. The child, when she's born, sues the clinicians involved for her deafness. 'But you wouldn't have existed if you hadn't been deaf,' they retort. A drug is available which, if taken in pregnancy, gives the child a lifelong immunity to all types of cancer. The parents refuse to take it. The child develops cancer and sues the parents. A doctor engages in a project to produce bionic soldiers who can run faster, jump higher, and see in the dark. Should he be stopped? What's the difference in principle between this sort of enhancement and the provision of a hip prosthesis to an elderly, arthritic woman? A doctor prescribes cognitive enhancement drugs to a university student about to sit her exams. They will allow her to revise for much longer. Should that be allowed? What if they're very expensive drugs, so that their prescription will mean that rich students do better in their exams? Is there anything wrong with genetic cognitive enhancement which increases the IQ of the subject by 50 points? If there is, does that mean that it's wrong to buy your child private education which will have the effect of multiplying the number of neuronal connections in his brain so that he has a cognitive advantage? And so on.

That's an exhilarating in-tray.

Cases discussed

Where cases are mentioned in the body of the text, the year given is that of the report cited in this section. That year is sometimes not the year that the case itself was decided. The authoritative law reports sometimes take a significant time to emerge.

Chapter 1: Origins and legacies

Bolam v Friern Hospital Management Committee [1957] 1 WLR 583
Airedale NHS Trust v Bland [1993] AC 789

Chapter 3: Before birth

ELH and PBH v United Kingdom (1998) 25 EHRR CD 158
R (Mellor) v Secretary of State for the Home Department [2002] QB 13
R v Human Fertilisation and Embryology Authority ex p Blood [1997] 2 WLR 806
Evans v United Kingdom (2006) 1 FCR 585
Planned Parenthood of Central Missouri v Danforth (1976) 96 S Ct 2831
C v S [1988] QB 135
Paton v United Kingdom (1981) 3 EHRR 408
Attorney General's Reference (No. 3 of 1994) [1998] AC 245
Winnipeg Child and Family Services (Northwest Area) v G (1997) 3 BHRC 611
Paton v Trustees of the British Pregnancy Advisory Services [1979] QB 276

St George's NHS Trust v S [1998] 3 All ER 673

Vo v France [2004] 2 FCR 526

Roe v Wade (1973) 410 US 113

McKay v Essex Area Health Authority [1982] QB 1166

McFarlane v Tayside Health Board [2000] AC 59

Doe v Bolton (1993) 410 US 179

Quintavalle (on behalf of Comment on Reproductive Ethics) v Human Fertilisation and Embryology Authority [2005] 2 AC 561

Chapter 4: Confidentiality and privacy

R v Department of Health, ex p Source Informatics Ltd [2000] Lloyd's Rep Med 76

Z v Finland (1998) 25 EHRR 371

Campbell v MGN [2004] 2 AC 457

W v Egdell [1990] 1 Ch 359

Jaffee v Redmond 518 US 1 (1996)

Tarasoff et al v The Regents of the University of California (1976) 17 Cal (3d) 358

Palmer v South Tees Health Authority [1999] Lloyd's Rep Med 151

R (Axon) v Secretary of State for Health [2006] QB 539

Lewis v Secretary of State for Health [2008] EWHC 2196

Chapter 5: Consent

R v Brown [1994] 1 AC 212

Laskey, Jaggard and Brown v UK (1997) 24 EHRR 39

Schloendorff v Society of New York Hospital (1914) 211 NY 125

Malette v Shulman (1990) 67 DLR (4th) 321

Gillick v West Norfolk and Wisbech Area Health Authority [1986] 1 AC 112

Prince v Massachusetts (1944) 321 US 158

R v Mobilio [1991] 1 VR 339

R v Clarence (1888) 22 QBD 23

R v Dica [2004] 1 QB 1257

Salgo v Leland Stanford Jr University Board of Trustees (1957) 154 Cal App 2d 560

Canterbury v Spence (1972) 464 2d 772

Reibl v Hughes (1980) 2 SCR 894

Rogers v Whittaker (1992) 175 CLR 479

Sidaway v Board of Governors of the Bethlem Royal Hospital and the
    Maudsley Hospital [1985] 1 AC 171
Pearce v United Bristol Healthcare NHS Trust [1999] PIQR P 53

Chapter 6: Clinical negligence

Donoghue v Stevenson (sub nom McAlister v Stevenson) [1932] AC
    562
Caparo Industries plc v Dickman [1990] 2 AC 605
Kapfunde v Abbey National plc [1999] 2 Lloyd's Rep Med 48
Goodwill v British Pregnancy Advisory Services [1996] 2 All ER 161
Tarasoff v The Regents of the University of California (supra)
Palmer v South Tees Health Authority (supra)
Bolam v Friern Hospital Management Committee (supra)
Bolitho v City and Hackney Health Authority [1998] AC 232
Sidaway v Board of Governors of the Bethlem Royal Hospital (supra)
Canterbury v Spence (supra)
Reibl v Hughes (supra)
F v R (1983) 33 SASR 189 (FC)
Castell v De Greef (1994) (4) SA 408
Rogers v Whittaker (supra)
Chaplin v Hicks [1911] 2 KB 786
Bailey v Ministry of Defence [2009] 1 WLR 1052
McGhee v National Coal Board [1973] 1 WLR 1
Chester v Afshar [2005] 1 AC 134

Chapter 8: Resource allocation

R v Cambridge Health Authority ex p B [1995] 1 WLR 898
Airedale NHS Trust v Bland (supra)

Chapter 9: The end of life

Airedale NHS Trust v Bland (supra)
R v Cox (1992) unreported
B v An NHS Trust [2002] 2 All ER 449
Satz v Perlmutter 379 So.2d 359 (Fla.1980)
McKay v Bergstedt (1990) 801 P. 2d 617
Georgia v McAfee (1989) 259 Ga. 579 (385 SE2d 651)

Chapter 10: Organ donation and the ownership of body parts

R v Bentham [2005] 2 WLR 384

R v Kelly [1999] QB 621

Doodeward v Spence (1908) 6 CLR 406

Moore v Regents of the University of California (1990) 793 P 2d 479

Hecht v Superior Court for Los Angeles County (1993) 20 Cal Rptr 2d
    275

R v Human Fertilisation and Embryology Authority ex p Blood
    (supra)

Evans v Amicus Healthcare: see Evans v United Kingdom (supra)

Yearworth v North Bristol NHS Trust [2010] QB 1

Diamond v Chakrabarty (1980) 447 US 303

Chapter 11: The future of medical law

Bolam v Friern Hospital Management Committee (supra)

Further reading

General

Margaret Brazier and Emma Cave, *Medicine, Patients and the Law* (London: Penguin, 2011)

Peter de Cruz, *Comparative Healthcare Law* (London: Cavendish, 2001)

Charles Foster, *Human Dignity in Bioethics and Law* (Oxford: Hart, 2011)

Andrew Grubb, Judith Laing, and Jean McHale (eds), *Principles of Medical Law*, 3rd edn (Oxford: Oxford University Press, 2010)

Jonathan Herring, *Medical Law and Ethics*, 3rd edn (Oxford: Oxford University Press, 2010)

Emily Jackson, *Medical Law: Text Cases and Materials*, 2nd edn (Oxford: Oxford University Press, 2009)

J. Kenyon Mason and Graeme T. Laurie, *Law and Medical Ethics*, 8th edn (Oxford: Oxford University Press, 2011)

Sean Pattinson, *Medical Law and Ethics*, 3rd edn (London: Sweet & Maxwell, 2011)

Chapter 1: Origins and legacies

E. Wicks (2009) 'Religion, Law and Medicine', *Medical Law Review* 17(3), 410

Chapter 2: The enforcement of medical law

See the general further reading list.

Chapter 3: Before birth

A. Alghrani and M. Brazier (2011) 'What is it? Whose is it? Repositioning the fetus in the context of research' *Cambridge Law Journal* 70: 51

Ronald Dworkin, *Life's Dominion: An Argument about Abortion and Euthanasia* (London: HarperCollins, 1993)

J. Finnis (1973) 'The rights and wrongs of abortion', *Philosophy and Public Affairs* (2) 117

Jonathan Herring, 'The Loneliness Of Status: The Legal And Moral Significance Of Birth', in F. Ebtehaj, J. Herring, M. Johnson, and M. Richards, *Birth Rites and Rights* (Oxford: Hart, 2011)

Kirsty Horsey and Hazel Biggs, *Human Fertilization and Embryology* (London: UCL Press, 2006)

Emily Jackson, *Regulating Reproduction* (Oxford: Hart, 2001)

Christopher Kaczor, *The Ethics of Abortion: Women's Rights, Human Life and the Question of Justice* (Abingdon: Routledge, 2010)

Rosamund Scott, *Rights, Duties and the Body: Law and Ethics of the Maternal–Fetal Conflict* (Oxford: Hart, 2002)

Rosamund Scott, *Choosing Possible Lives: Law and Ethics of Prenatal and Pre-implantation Genetic Diagnosis* (Oxford: Hart Publishing, 2007)

John Spencer and Antje Du Bois-Pedain (eds), *Freedom and Responsibility in Reproductive Choice* (Oxford: Hart, 2006)

Michael Tooley, Celia Wolf-Devine, Philip Devine, and Alison Jaggar, *Abortion: Three Perspectives* (Oxford: Oxford University Press, 2009)

Chapter 4: Confidentiality and privacy

Bridgit Dimond, *Legal Aspects of Patient Confidentiality* (London/Salisbury: Quay, 2010)

General Medical Council, *Good Medical Practice* (London: GMC, 2006)

General Medical Council, *Guidance on Confidentiality* (London: GMC, 2009)

Graeme Laurie, *Genetic Privacy* (Cambridge: Cambridge University Press, 2002)

William Lowrance, *Privacy, Confidentiality and Health Research* (Cambridge: Cambridge University Press, 2012)

Heather Widdows and Caroline Mullen, *The Governance of Genetic Information: Who Decides?* (Cambridge: Cambridge University Press, 2009)

Chapter 5: Consent

Christopher Johnston (ed.), *Medical Treatment: Decisions and the Law* (London: Bloomsbury, 2009)

Mary Donnelly, *Healthcare Decision-Making and the Law: Autonomy, Capacity and the Limits of Liberalism* (Cambridge: Cambridge University Press, 2010)

Alasdair Maclean, *Autonomy, Informed Consent and Medical Law: A Relational Challenge* (Cambridge: Cambridge University Press, 2009)

Sheila MacLean, *Autonomy, Consent and the Law* (Abingdon: Routledge, 2009)

Chapter 6: Clinical negligence

Lara Khoury, *Uncertain Causation in Medical Liability* (Oxford: Hart, 2006)

Marc Stauch, *The Law of Medical Negligence in England and Germany: A Comparative Analysis* (Oxford: Hart, 2008)

R. Mulheron (2010) 'Trumping *Bolam*: A Critical Legal Analysis of *Bolitho*'s "Gloss"', *Cambridge Law Journal* 69: 609

Chapter 7: Research on human subjects

Hazel Biggs, *Healthcare Research Ethics and Law: Regulation, Review and Responsibility* (Abingdon: Routledge-Cavendish, 2009)

Philip Cheung, *Public Trust in Medical Research? Ethics, Law and Accountability* (London: Radcliffe, 2007)

Ruth Macklin, *Double Standards in Medical Research in Developing Countries* (Cambridge: Cambridge University Press, 2004)

Aurora Plomer, *The Law and Ethics of Medical Research: International Bioethics and Human Rights* (Abingdon: Routledge-Cavendish, 2005)

Chapter 8: Resource allocation

Charles Camosy, *Too Expensive to Treat?—Finitude, Tragedy, and the Neonatal ICU* (Grand Rapids, MI: Eerdmans, 2010)

Y. Denier (2008) 'Mind the Gap! Three Approaches to Scarcity in Health Care', *Medicine, Health Care and Philosophy* 11: 73

Christopher Newdick, *Who Should we Treat? Rights, Rationing, and Resources in the NHS* (Oxford: Oxford University Press, 2005)

Keith Syrett, *Law, Legitimacy and the Rationing of Healthcare* (Cambridge: Cambridge University Press, 2007)

Chapter 9: The end of life

Hazel Biggs, *Euthanasia, Death with Dignity and the Law* (Oxford: Hart, 2001)

Ronald Dworkin, *Life's Dominion* (London: HarperCollins, 1993)

Jonathan Glover, *Causing Death and Saving Lives* (London: Penguin, 1990)

Richard Huxtable, *Euthanasia, Ethics and the Law: From Conflict to Compromise* (Abingdon: Routledge-Cavendish, 2007)

Richard Huxtable, *Law, Ethics and Compromise at the Limits of Life: To Treat or not to Treat* (Abingdon: Routledge-Cavendish, 2012)

Emily Jackson and John Keown, *Debating Euthanasia* (Oxford: Hart, 2011)

John Keown (ed.), *Euthanasia Examined* (Cambridge: Cambridge University Press, 1995)

John Keown (ed.), *Euthanasia, Ethics and Public Policy* (Cambridge: Cambridge University Press, 2002)

Penney Lewis, *Assisted Dying and Legal Change* (Oxford: Oxford University Press, 2007)

A. Maclean (2008) 'Advance Directives and Anticipatory Decision-Making', *Medical Law Review* 1

Sheila McLean, *Assisted Dying: Reflections on the Need to Reform* (Abingdon: Routledge, 2007)

Mary Warnock and Elisabeth Macdonald, *Easeful Death: Is there a Case for Assisted Dying?* (Oxford: Oxford University Press, 2009)

Chapter 10: Organ donation and the ownership of body parts

Richard Hardcastle, *Law and the Human Body* (Oxford: Hart, 2007)

David Price, *Human Tissue in Transplantation and Research: A Modal Legal and Ethical Framework* (Cambridge: Cambridge University Press, 2009)

Stephen Wilkinson, *Bodies for Sale: Ethics and Exploitation in the Human Body Trade* (London: Routledge, 2003)

T. M. Wilkison, *Ethics and the Acquisition of Organs* (Oxford: Oxford University Press, 2011)

Index

Expand your collection of
VERY SHORT INTRODUCTIONS